Ecologies in Southeast Asian Literatures
Histories, Myths and Societies

Edited by

Chi Pham
Institute of Literature, Vietnam Academy of Social Sciences, Vietnam

Chitra Sankaran
National University of Singapore, Singapore

Gurpreet Kaur
The University of Warwick

Series in Literary Studies

Copyright © 2020 by the Authors

All rights reserved. No part of this publication may be reproduced, stored in a retrieval system, or transmitted in any form or by any means, electronic, mechanical, photocopying, recording, or otherwise, without the prior permission of Vernon Art and Science Inc.

www.vernonpress.com

In the Americas:
Vernon Press
1000 N West Street,
Suite 1200, Wilmington,
Delaware 19801
United States

In the rest of the world:
Vernon Press
C/Sancti Espiritu 17,
Malaga, 29006
Spain

Series in Literary Studies

Library of Congress Control Number: 2019934217

ISBN: 978-1-62273-785-7

Also available: 978-1-62273-633-1 [Hardback]; 978-1-62273-683-6 [PDF, E-Book]

Product and company names mentioned in this work are the trademarks of their respective owners. While every care has been taken in preparing this work, neither the authors nor Vernon Art and Science Inc. may be held responsible for any loss or damage caused or alleged to be caused directly or indirectly by the information contained in it.

Every effort has been made to trace all copyright holders, but if any have been inadvertently overlooked the publisher will be pleased to include any necessary credits in any subsequent reprint or edition.

Cover's image by Sasin Tipchai, Pixabay.

Cover design by Vernon Press.

Table of Contents

Bonding ASEAN together through Literary Studies, Ecological Criticism and the Environmental Humanities   1

   Chi P. Pham,
   Institute of Literature,
   Vietnam Academy of Social Sciences, Vietnam

   Chitra Sankaran,
   National University of Singapore, Singapore

   Gupreet Kaur

Chapter 1
Orangutans: Myth, Metaphor and Survival   9

   Helen Tiffin,
   University of Wollongong, Australia

Chapter 2
Imaginings of Disasters in two Southeast Asian Narratives: Trauma, Risk and Management   21

   Chitra Sankaran,
   National University of Singapore, Singapore

Chapter 3
Georgic Gastronomies: Restorative Eating in the Anthropocene with Margaret Atwood and Merlinda Bobis   33

   Jose Monfred C. Sy,
   University of the Philippines, Philippines

Chapter 4
A Return to Innocence: Encountering the Numinous in Children's Fantasy Fiction by Cyan Abad-Jugo   49

   Gabriela Lee,
   University of the Philippines, Philippines

Chapter 5
"Escaping from the Anxiety, Returning to the Field":
Nostalgia in Nguyen Quang Thieu's Ecological Poems   59
    Dang Thi Bich Hong,
    Hung Vuong University, Vietnam

Chapter 6
Humorous revalorisation of traditional farming
in some contemporary Vietnamese literary works   73
    Hoang To Mai,
    Institute of Literature, Vietnam Academy of Social Sciences, Vietnam

Chapter 7
Environmental Losses of Urbanisation:
Reading Eco-Narratives of Đỗ Phấn   87
    Le Thi Huong Thuy,
    Vietnam Institute of Literature, Vietnam

Chapter 8
Imagining Vietnam from the War Years
to Post-war Period in *Nhiệt đới gió mùa/*
***The tropical monsoon* by Lê Minh Khuê:**
Templates for Ecological Narrative and Beyond   99
    Nguyen Thi Nhu Trang,
    Vietnam National University, Vietnam

Chapter 9
Nature and Humans in Sino-Vietnamese
conceptions and practices. Articulations
between Asian vernacular "analogism" and
Western modern "naturalism" ontologies   111
    Christian Culas,
    French National Center for Scientific Research (CNRS), Centre Norbert Elias, EHESS, France

Chapter 10
Tales from the Mouth of the River:
Ecocritical Mythology and Philippine Epic Poetry   129
    Timothy F. Ong,
    University of the Philippines, Philippines

Chapter 11
**Animism in Southeast Asian Myths and Its
Impacts on Acts of Environmental Protection**   141
Nguyen Thi Mai Lien,
Ha Noi National University of Education, Vietnam

Bionotes of Contributors   155

Index   159

Bonding ASEAN together through Literary Studies, Ecological Criticism and the Environmental Humanities

Chi P. Pham,
Institute of Literature, Vietnam Academy of Social Sciences, Vietnam

Chitra Sankaran,
National University of Singapore, Singapore

Gupreet Kaur

The Association of Southeast Asian Nations or ASEAN is a regional intergovernmental organisation that includes ten Southeast Asian countries: Indonesia, Malaysia, the Philippines, Singapore, Thailand, Brunei, Cambodia, Laos, Myanmar and Vietnam. While the foremost reason for creating this organisation was the facilitation of economic, political, security (military), educational and sociocultural interests, the environment is increasingly making its importance known within the organisation. While, arguably, the region's most high-profile environmental issue has been tackling haze pollution, the twenty-first century is seeing other pressing environmental concerns within the ASEAN region as well.[1] For example, deforestation, with Indonesia recording the largest loss of forested area in the region; plastic waste dumping, where five member states have been consistently ranked high in plastic waste pollution (as the region sees a high rate of tourism); threatened plant, fish and animal species; trash dumping from foreign countries such as Canada and Japan, which ASEAN has yet to resolve.

With such pressing environmental concerns within the region, there has been a concurrent rise in literary works centring environmental concerns. In response to this, the Association for the Study of Literature and the Environment-Association of Southeast Asian Nations (ASLE-ASEAN) was set up in 2016 in Singapore, with the inaugural workshop being held in

---

[1] ASEAN facilitated an agreement to tackle haze pollution in the year 2002, called the ASEAN Agreement on Transboundary Haze Pollution.

August 2016 at the National University of Singapore. The second ASLE-ASEAN conference was held in Vietnam in 2018 at the Vietnam National University in Hanoi. Through these conferences, several environmental issues within the literatures of the ASEAN region were discussed, and the second ASLE-ASEAN conference in 2018 raised issues that were not only particular to the ASEAN region but also have global implications. One has to keep in mind that though the ASEAN region is diverse economically, politically, culturally and linguistically, the environment in its broadest sense plays a crucial role in binding the region. This can be witnessed through the November 2017 ASEAN Conference on Reducing Marine Debris in ASEAN Region, held in Phuket, Thailand. At this conference, the head of the United Nations Environment Programme's Coral Reef Unit, Jerker Tamelander, remarked that "[i]t's clear now that this region is probably the single largest contributor of plastic litter into the marine environment in the world, which means that if we want to solve the marine litter problem as a global challenge, we have to solve it in this region" (quoted in Kaur, Web Source), highlighting the critical global importance of ASEAN's initiatives to tackle its environmental problems.[2]

Ecocriticism in relation to the Southeast Asian region is relatively new. So far, John Charles Ryan's *Ecocriticism in Southeast Asia* is the first book of its kind to focus on the region and its literature to give an ecocritical analysis. Published in January 2018, this edited volume compiles analyses of the eco-literatures from most of the Southeast Asian region. This volume provides us with a broad insight into the ecological concerns of the region as depicted in its literatures and other cultural texts. The current volume will go further to focus specifically on the prominent myths and histories and the myriad ways they connect to the social fabric of the region. Our book is an original contribution to the field in highlighting the mytho-historical basis of many of the region's literatures and their relationship to the environment.

It is important to recognise the fact that any attempt to cogently distil a holistic ecocritical and ecological imagination relevant to the Southeast Asian geo-space necessitates recognising the great cultural heterogeneity of the region and especially the diverse environmental cultures of its diverse ethnopolitical groups. Environmental cultures cannot be separated from myths and histories. Furthermore, while discussing myths

---

[2] See: Satwant Kaur, "Tackling Plastic Pollution Priority at ASEAN Meeting", UN Environment, <https://www.unenvironment.org/news-and-stories/story/tackling-plastic-pollution-priority-asean-meeting>.

and histories, what gets foregrounded is the idea of continuity that comes with residing in a place, what Greg Garrard terms 'dwelling'. As Garrard stresses, this is not a temporary or transient state but implies the "long-term imbrication of humans in a landscape of memory, ancestry and death, of ritual, life and work." (p. 108). Thus 'dwelling' and the landscape of memory cannot and should not be disentangled. ASEAN nations like many other such political groupings of neighboring countries share a common landscape of memory even while retaining their unique histories and myths.

For one, several ASEAN countries share a common Sino-Indic ancestry, which emerges in the predominance of Buddhism in the region, with the subtle but pervasive influence of Hinduism that can be identified even in the native cultures of pre-Islamic Indonesia and Malaysia. The harking back to myth and teasing out its connection to history becomes an important exercise in environmental consciousness-raising. This occurs in many ways. Firstly, it makes us ponder about the stereotype of the harmonious, pre-political native, who supposedly lived in harmony with nature. Human history, as far back as we can go, appears to have been filled with violence and conflict. Therefore, one needs to understand that ideas of harmony, whether environmental or otherwise, need to be questioned and qualified. Simultaneously, however, one also needs to understand the importance and usefulness of myths and indigenous histories that offer an alter-vision to one increasingly driven by global capitalism and individual gain.

The political philosopher Murray Bookchin describes the concept of 'social ecology' in his book, *The Ecology of Freedom* (1982). Here, he emphasises the idea that ecological problems are caused by human social problems and they can be resolved only by reorganising society among ecological and ethical lines. Social ecologists therefore emphasise the importance of studying the myths and ideologies that are manifested in societies since they believe that these will lead to a clearer understanding of the reasons for the ecological problems that beset them. This idea becomes important to our current study.

The articles in this volume, varied though they are, together explore the idea of nature and its relationship with humans. The always problematic questions that surround such explorations, such as, "why do we regard nature as 'external'?" or "how is humankind a continuum with nature?" emerge throughout the volume either overtly or implicitly. As Pepper (1993) points out, what Karl Marx referenced as 'first' or 'external' nature, gave rise to humankind. But humanity "worked on this 'first' nature to produce a 'second' nature: the material creations of society plus its institutions, ideas and values." (Pepper, 108). Thus, our volume constantly negotiates this field of ideas and belief systems, in diverse ways and in various cultures, attempting to relate them to the current ecological predicaments of ASEAN.

Summary of Chapters

The individual contributions to this collection which, with some exceptions, are mostly based on primary texts that emerge from ASEAN, touch on a range of environmental issues. A variety of themes, ranging from human-animal exchanges, trauma, risk and management, food security, myths and legends in children's literature, nostalgia, war and post-war, postcolonial ecocriticism, dirty aesthetics, the combination of eco-narratives, a Vietnamese constitution of nature and humans, are touched on.

Helen Tiffin writes about orangutans that are found in the wild in Southeast Asia. She interrogates how fiction explores their decreasing numbers in the wild, and how it can contribute to the survival of this species. In her essay, she raises questions regarding what "narratives, myths, stereotypes, have been important" and "how these have changed during the last two centuries." Her article examines how these narratives have influenced human (especially Western) perceptions of orangutans and highlights their current plight as a radically endangered species. Her paper elaborates on ways through which some contemporary writers are now using fiction in order to draw attention to the plight of the currently endangered population.

Chitra Sankaran uses the concepts of risk and management as an intellectual paradigm to manage the environmental crises and threats in the daily lives of the diverse ASEAN populations. Sankaran's essay shows that through narrativising and imagining disasters, trauma and risk can be coded and interpreted, and therefore managed. Sankaran uses two narratives from Vietnam and Myanmar that imagine and narrate environmental disasters. Both narratives, being rooted in their national histories, highlight the scope of risk and its management through an ecocritical reading. As such, Sankaran's essay brings forth the idea of a gesture towards possible futures through unacknowledged pasts and national histories, where these environmental futures are "possibly unwanted" and also remain "within the spectrum of plausibility".

Jose Monfred C. Sy writes about the issue of food security in the age of the Anthropocene. Sy sees the Anthropocene as food-driven, where "food becomes a major driver of environmental change". Using the tools of environmental justice and highlighting the food-related crises experienced today due to neoliberal geopolitics, Sy analyses Margaret Atwood's *Oryx and Crake* and *The Year of the Flood*, and Merlinda Bobis' *Locust Girl: A Lovesong* to show that "these narratives destabilise the perverted conception of food in our era".

Sy's essay reflects the ongoing issues of food security that the ASEAN region faces. ASEAN member states recognise the importance of strengthening food security to maintain stability, peace and prosperity throughout the region, and to that effect held The World Food Summit in the year 1996. Food security was defined in the summit as "existing when all people at all times have access to sufficient, safe, nutritious food to maintain a healthy and active life".[3]

Gabriela Lee writes about children's literature in the Philippines, and the use of supernatural and fantastical elements which the child protagonists use to overcome social and physical limitations. These children then impact their immediate environments in empowering ways. Using the concept of the "numinous" by Brawley, Palumbo and Sullivan, Lee analyses Filipino writer Cyan Abad-Jugo's collection of short stories to show how myths and legends are retold for a contemporary generation and re-tooled so that "today's children may begin their own transformations".

Dang Thi Bich Hong discusses the use of nostalgia in Vietnamese poet Nguyen Quang Thieu's ecological poems. Hong writes that the poet makes use of a nostalgic past and desire to show the environmental problems the region is facing today, and how the poet brings out the changes in modern society via the use of metaphors of anxiety and the field.

Hoang To Mai uses the idea of 'dirty aesthetics' to re-read Vietnamese contemporary literary works, Y Ban's *Hoya* and Nguyen Huy Thiep's *Mr. Mong's Story*. Mai proposes that these texts, though not written with the specific intention of an environmentally-friendly reading, nonetheless offer important insights into the ecological problems Vietnam is facing in contemporary times and uses humorous revalorisation of traditional farming within the texts to show this.

Le Thi Huong Thuy, relying on literary analysis and context analysis, examines Đỗ Phấn's representation of environmental destruction and other potential ecological risks as consequences of urbanising processes in Vietnam. The paper demonstrates that Đỗ Phấn's ecological stories embody

---

[3] See: World Health Organization, "Food Security", <http://www.who.int/trade/glossary/story028/en/>.

a deep sense among Vietnamese intellectuals of their responsibility for the national project of urbanising existing cities and countryside areas and for ecological issues. Moreover, the ways through which Đỗ Phấn's stories address and attend Vietnamese public concerns over environmental costs and associated social problems that had particularly emerged since the Reform (1986) indicate the on-going practical role of ecological literature in political and social lives of Vietnam.

Nguyen Thi Nhu Trang uses Vietnamese writer Lê Minh Khuê's collection of short stories "The Tropical Monsoon" to show the narrative templates of 'Eco'. Trang proposes that the combination of 'Eco' in world narratives and Vietnamese narratives contributes to "the shift in the image of Vietnam from a country mired in war to post-war" and shows how the writer emphasises peace and harmony in the lives of individuals and the nation.

Christian Culas writes how Vietnam is trying to establish ideas of what constitutes nature and the relations between humans and non-humans. Culas uses a three-pronged approach to reconstruct the conceptions of humans and nature: (1) an historical overview of the conceptions of human/nature and human/human, (2) a hybrid way of thought and action which merges the traditional Chinese mode of worldview and the Western mode of worldview, and (3) what nature means in Sino-Vietnamese conceptions and practices that show the diversity of how nature is perceived and acted upon. Culas uses examples from Taoist conceptions of nature, the integration of man and nature through consumption, and Vietnamese conceptions of a 'nature garden'.

Timothy Ong's essay looks at how folk narratives interrogate the possibility of inquiring about the relationship of humans with the world through the mythology instantiated by folk poetics. He looks at the epic poem from Central Philippines entitled "Hinilawod" that is framed with and against nature. Ong's essay ultimately provides a way to reimagine and reconstruct indigenous epistemologies in Philippine folk texts from an ecocritical/ecophilosophical lens through a riverine discourse in the poem.

Nguyen Thi Mai Lien examines the ideas of animism in the myths of Southeast Asia and its impacts on environmental behaviours of ancient tribes in Southeast Asians. The paper also wonders whether animism is still alive today and, if so, how it can offer deep lessons for contemporary people regarding the protection of the environment.

The Importance of ASEAN Literatures and Environment

This collection of essays is important in not only bringing to prominence the ASEAN region, its literatures and environment, but also in highlighting how our perception of the environment is culturally shaped through language and literature. While such literature reflects cultural values, it also resists them.

It is our hope that through this collection of essays, certain absolutes which form the foundation of our unconscious biases are challenged. These essays, by employing concepts such as hybridity, interdependency, and human and non-human exchanges, interrogate both the world that already exists and the comforting anthropocentric paradigms that humans are comfortable existing within.

Thinking about the environment through literature then allows us, as readers and writers, to imagine new worlds where it is important to re-think certain bedrock assumptions such as responsibility, action and selfhood, whether human or non-human, and to give expression to new cultural possibilities.

Works Cited

Bookchin, Murray. *The Ecology of Freedom: The Emergence and Dissolution of Hierarchy.* Palo Alto: Cheshire Books, 1982.

Garrard, Greg. *Ecocriticism;* The New Critical Idiom Series. London & New York: Routledge, 2004.

Kaur, Satwant. "Tackling Plastic Pollution Priority at ASEAN Meeting". *UN Environment.* Available at <https://www.unenvironment.org/news-and-stories/story/tackling-plastic-pollution-priority-asean-meeting>. Accessed 6 July 2018.

Pepper, David. *Eco-Socialism: From Deep Ecology to Social Justice.* London: Routledge, 1993.

Ryan, John Charles. *Southeast Asian Ecocriticism: Theories, Practices, Prospects.* Lanham: Lexington Books, 2018.

World Health Organization. "Food Security". Available at <http://www.who.int/trade/glossary/story028/en/>. Accessed on 6 July 2018.

Chapter 1

Orangutans:
Myth, Metaphor and Survival

Helen Tiffin,
University of Wollongong, Australia

Abstract

Orangutans are found in the wild only in South East Asia, in Sumatra and Borneo, and their numbers are decreasing every year. In what ways might fiction contribute to their survival? Humans have always found monkeys, especially primates, "good to think with", not least about their own humanity and its positive and negative aspects. What narratives, myths and stereotypes have been important, and how have these changed during the last two centuries? How have these narratives influenced human (especially Western) perceptions of orangutans and their current plight as a radically endangered species? This paper considers some ways in which the figure of the orangutan has been used in influential writing of the last two centuries, and the ways in which some contemporary writers are now using fiction in order to draw attention to the plight of the currently endangered population.

Key Words: orangutans; fiction; monkeys; conservation; animal stereotypes.

Can literature, which is clearly important in influencing perceptions of animals (and constructing animal stereotypes) also help in contributing to their survival? The direct effects of literature on the survival (or extinction) of particular animal groups is not, of course, quantifiable. But we do know, for instance, that literature can effect major changes in public perception and public sentiment (Harriet Beecher Stowe's *Uncle Tom's Cabin* is an obvious example). The orangutan is found naturally nowhere else on earth outside South East Asia: in Borneo and Sumatra.[1] (As reported in *New Scientist* (14), a new species of orangutan has been recently discovered in Sumatra — but its "discovery", in an irony far too typical of present times — coincides with a warning of its imminent extinction and that of the other two species in Malaysia and Indonesia).

Monkeys and apes, particularly the Great Apes, have a long history in Western literary representation, while their influence in Bornean and Sumatran legend and myth is much less significant, and has often, but not always, shown to have itself been influenced by Western accounts, particularly in English and French.[2] This western interest in monkeys and apes is usually ascribed to their position on the borderline between human and animal. They exist, as Donna Harraway has aptly put it, "at the dangerous edge of the garden of nature" (Harraway 126) and in this unique position they can represent human traits, both good and bad, act as commentators on human behaviour or be used to satirise human folly.

This essay briefly considers examples of these genres in the Western tradition, the stereotypes of orangutans (both good and bad) that have been employed in fiction, as well as the ways in which writers have used fictional orangutans to comment on human behaviour. In contemporary writing, however, orangutans appear less as human satirists or mere *metaphors* for humans than as educators who attempt to curb our destructive greed, demonstrating the havoc we have wrecked on their (and our own) environments. They also no longer appear as "stand-ins" for us but as beings in their own right whose lives are now under grave threat of extinction *because* of us.

During the eighteenth century, the orangutan began to appear in plays and novels, and later in short stories. Most of the early authors had not seen an orangutan, even in captivity, but the writings of travellers and scientists were so widely circulated, the illustrations (of Bontius and Tulp) so often redrawn, and public displays of orangutan-like creatures so common, that a knowledge of the term "orangutan" and a sense of what it stood for was widespread within the literate elite of western Europe by the second half of the eighteenth century. The fiction writers who drew on this public knowledge, with all its inconsistencies, were not primarily concerned with presenting an accurate portrait of the orangutan in terms

---

[1] For more details, please see *Wild Man from Borneo: A Cultural History of the Orangutan* by Robert Cribb, Helen Gilbert and Helen Tiffin. Many sections of the paper draw on, or have been published in it.

[2] See Cribb et al for further detail.

of the scientific and philosophical discourses of the day. Rather, they saw in the ape's close resemblance to humans an opportunity to explore aspects of the human condition in a new way. They were also in a position to ask awkward questions that scientists often did not and to imagine possibilities beyond the protocols of the scientific method.

Until the first half of the nineteenth century, scientists commonly used the term "orangutan" to refer to all great apes. Many fictional great apes are thus composites of imagery and information relating to gorillas and chimpanzees, and sometimes monkeys and other apes, as well as to actual orangutans. There was also scientific uncertainty about the distribution of great apes. Therefore, it is to be expected that fiction writers also use the term loosely and locate their animals in a wide variety of warm, exotic places: India, Southeast Asia, South America, Angola, the Cape, Africa in general, or the South Pacific. Neither Western science nor the Western intellectual world in general had any clear idea of ecology. Representation of apes and monkeys in Western writing had a long genealogy, stretching back at least to the Greek classics, and these simian stereotypes necessarily inflect eighteenth-century writing about orangutans. The "orangutans" of earlier fictional works frequently became a composite or selective reference point for subsequent depictions, so that themes developed by one writer found new (and sometimes not so new) expression in later literature. Changes in attitudes to human relations with other primates were thus reciprocally interwoven with changes in modes of writing, pictorial representation and exhibition. Fictional accounts in general retain a readership much longer than do most scientific works. Once the distinct character of orangutans was scientifically settled in the 1830s, no-one read Tyson or Camper for their science; the works of the scientists who superseded them were in turn eclipsed by later research. But by contrast, some fictional works featuring orangutans continue to attract readers and generate insights and impressions today, carrying striking images and narratives from one century to the next.

Apes had traditionally been used in fable and fiction to tell Western societies something about themselves. In some cases, simians write or speak in order to impart insights to the West; in others, their actions are used to illuminate generally negative features of Western societies, in much the same way as monkeys of all kinds had been used in previous eras.

One example, typical of this era, is the so-called "Boston orangutan" whose critique of human behaviour arises from her experience of having been captured and transported to America where she has — like a number of actual eighteenth-century orangutans — been put on display. Her critique is contained in a "letter" to her friend in Java. Whereas, she notes, orangutans "partake sparingly of the fruits most liberally dispensed ... by the influences of a delightful climate and the perpetual vegetation of the tropics", man by contrast "cannot make a single meal without some exhibition of his cannibal propensities", greedily demolishing "some other animal as good as he to satiate his raging appetite" ("The Orang Outang" 498). This, notes the orangutan, is particularly hypocritical when human philosophers continually recommend moderation but do not practice what they preach. "Appetite and accumulation," she writes, characterise human society. Humans pride themselves on their "gift of speech", forgetting "in their vainglory that the same gift is enjoyed by the parrot and cockatoo". But since their philosophers (contradictorily) trumpet silence as a virtue, "how superior in moral dignity is the Orang-Outang who practises this virtue on principle, and on all occasions, to the man or woman who would rather die outright than hold his or her tongue for half an hour" (498-499). Strangely, too, although man regards his noblest quality as the soul, he spends his life "engrossed by the care of the body" while his "soul" is "treated with so little ceremony that they have nothing, but what they call their own inward consciousness to vouch for its existence" (498), a circular testimony the orangutan scribe finds particularly unconvincing. Moreover, these "soul-and-body, want-multiplying, eternally talking people, have the impudence to call me ugly" (499).

The fictionalised orangutan, as in the commentary above, becomes in two classical nineteenth-century English works not only commentator on human society but an actual participant in it. Edgar Allan Poe's "Murders in the Rue Morgue" and Thomas Love Peacock's *Melincourt* still exert a strong influence today on human perceptions of orangutans, even though their depictions of the animal present completely opposite pictures.

In 1817, Thomas Love Peacock in his novel *Melincourt* created the unforgettable Sir Orang Haut-ton, a silent orangutan who participated fully in English society. Sir Orang is gentle, strong, educable, musical, contemplative, and genteel — excellent company, if lacking in conversation. *Melincourt*, the work in which he has become the de facto hero, has remained significant for its political satire and thinly disguised portraits of the Romantic poets and thinkers, as well as for its characterisation of Sir Oran, still often described as the most engaging picture of an orangutan in all literature.

Melincourt is a satire, attacking rotten boroughs (parliamentary seats controlled by local landowners), rural poverty, upper-class wealth, marriages in which monetary motives outweigh the meeting of minds and the introduction of paper money. The central plot of the novel is the making of a match between the chief character, Sylvan Forester, and Anthelia Melincourt, during which many obstacles emerge, some of which are overcome by the intervention of Sir Oran. This storyline provides a thin framework for a series of discussions between Forester and others, in which the taciturn Sir Oran plays no role but of which he is sometimes the subject. The approved opinions in the novel are those of the loquacious hero, Forester (a character based on the mature Percy Bysshe Shelley); his fiancée, Anthelia; and Mr Fax, a portrait of T. R. Malthus, celebrated for his powerful prognosis on the future of human populations. Sylvan Forester, a proto-conservationist, has Sir Oran as his constant companion. Through Forester, Anthelia, Fax, and the actions (rather than speech) of Sir Oran Haut-ton, Peacock appears to endorse Scottish philosopher Lord Monboddo's idea about the humanity of orangutans.

Peacock's portrait is an inspired literary device to castigate human cowardice, greed, and inequality and to lampoon the electoral system of an apparently "civilised" British society; in short, Sir Oran Haut-ton,[3] as "natural man", stands in marked contrast to urban sophistication and corruption. But he is much more than just a traditional novelistic device for satirising human follies. A different kind of human — but still very much a human — Sir Oran Haut-ton is stronger, more reliable, direct, and honest in his dealings with the upper-class company into which Forester has introduced him than are most of the other characters in the novel. Although he has acquired a baronetcy, plays the flute, rescues the heroine, and is elected to Parliament from the borough of Onevote, he never speaks, a lack for which his mentor and companion Forester amply compensates.[4]

---

[3] Haut-ton, meaning "High-toned". Even though Sir Oran-Haut-ton's origins are philosophic rather than geographical, it is worth noting that *Melincourt* is one of the earliest novels in which environmental questions are aired in the conversations between Forester and Fax. Though their environmental discussions and conclusion have nothing to do with orangutans, or forests outside England, they prefigure those fictions of the twentieth and twenty-first centuries wherein loss of orangutan habitat **is** linked to the issues Fax and Forester discuss: greed, and human overpopulation

[4] As readers, we have become conditioned to interpret thinking, talking animals in fiction as representing humans, or aspects of their behaviour. Only recently have some writers begun to portray animals as "speaking and thinking *in their own right*", deliberately incorporating devices to ensure we do not read the animals in their works allegorically.

A very different kind of orangutan from Sir Oran appears in a work credited with being the first ever detective story — Poe's "Murders in the Rue Morgue". A sailor brings an orangutan captured in the "Far East" to Paris with him. The orangutan escapes from custody, and, having watched his "master" shave his beard, takes the razor, scales a Paris apartment building and attempts to "shave" the hair from the two women he finds there. Inept at this, of course, his attempt is disastrous, the women are hysterical with terror, and the result is a double murder, whose circumstances confound the police after the orangutan escapes through the window. (They are of course looking for a human perpetrator.) Poe's proto-detective Dupin does however solve the case, setting in motion two enduring stereotypes: that of the "amateur" detective who can always outthink the local constabulary, and the dangerous (even murderous) orangutan.

Although both Peacock's and Poe's very different orangutans are not simple satirical critiques of human society, nor simple metaphors for a human trait (or traits), both are depicted in contexts which allow them to play pivotal roles in philosophical conflicts of the day: in Peacock's novel, as well as satirising the English political system, his portrait of Sir Oran Haut-ton plays a significant role in debates about the status of humans and the great apes. In the case of Poe's figuration, critics have speculated that the fierce, murderous figure, let loose, as it were on "civilised" Parisian society, buys into a racist fear of the abolition of slavery in the American south.[5]

The roles of the orangutans in the fictions of peacock and Poe are both very different from that in Pierre Boulle's *Monkey Planet (La planete des singes)*, 1963. Boulle's work imagines a reversal of dominance between human and non-human apes. The book, like *Melincourt*, not only remains in print in the twenty-first century but has been influential in its representations of orangutans, particularly through the iconic films based on Boulle's novel. The first of this film series, *Planet of the Apes* (1968), used human actors in ape costumes to depict the three species which control the "Monkey Planet": chimpanzees, orangutans and gorillas.

On the planet on which Ulysse Merou and his fellow voyagers land, the dominant structure of twentieth-century Earth has been reversed. Here the apes are the ones who are civilised and socially organised, while the humans are wild, degenerate "animals", deprived of any (human) dignity.

---

[5] See Maurice S. Lee, *Slavery, Philosophy, and American Literature 1830-1860*. Cambridge, Cambridge University Press, 2005.

The three groups of great apes — chimpanzees, orangutans and gorillas — wear clothes and between them run the planet. Naked humans roam wild in the forest, lacking any accoutrements of civilisation or, in the view of the apes (and Merou and his companions), any signs of an active intelligence. Their instincts (especially in relation to impending danger) are keen; they can make and use "primitive" tools, and have a limited degree of sociality. In short, the humans possess those attributes generally ascribed by us to the great apes, while those capacities accorded "humans" on earth are instead possessed, to different degrees, by the three "ape" species. Gorillas, the most militaristic and least intelligent, hunt humans for sport but also capture subjects for experiments — behavioural, anatomical, physiological, social and psychological — which are carried out by the most intelligent group, the chimpanzees, under the management of the more conservative and less innovative orangutans. Humans are subjected to various intelligence tests, almost always about problem-solving in relation to the acquisition of food, experiments not dissimilar to Wolfgang Kohler's on chimpanzees and orangutans early in the twentieth century, a telling critique of which is included in Nobel Prize winner J. M. Coetzee's groundbreaking novel *The Lives of Animals* (1999). Experimentation does not stop there in *Monkey Planet*, either. As with Kohler and other behavioural scientists, the chimpanzees and orangutans of Boulle's fictional world are interested in the sexual habits of their human captives as well as being involved in vivisecting them to learn more about these apparently "wild" ancestors, and thus about their own more evolutionary "primitive" selves.

Merou, the human visitor to the planet, is captured and placed in a cage with the beautiful but apparently vacuous Monkey Planet human, Nova. They eventually escape with the help of the chimpanzee scientists though not before Merou demonstrates intelligence, knowledge, and linguistic skills well surpassing those of the planet's "wild" humans. Nevertheless, it is a long struggle for Merou to have his capacities recognised and acknowledged. What is genuinely intelligent initiative on his part is persistently interpreted as merely a superior capacity for imitation; and rebellion against his incarceration is taken as further proof of savagery and lack of civilisation, while its alternative, apparent acceptance, is read as mindless apathy.

This reversal of dominance in Boulle's novel, its replication and critique of the ways we have treated the nonhuman apes, together with its exploration of the modes by which such dominant attitudes and practices, once naturalised, necessarily become self-fulfilling, self-sustaining, and self-serving, constitutes a stringent condemnation of our current treatment of other apes (and perhaps animals) generally. But interpretations of Boulle's work have tended to occlude this more obvious reading, particularly since the 1968 film version of the work is better known than the original novel. Among the most popular films ever made, *Planet of the Apes* and its successors, produced in the United States during the racial tensions of the 1970s and 1980s ensured that audiences would read a potentially interspecies text for its racial, rather than speciest critique.

In James Hall's 1995 novel, *Gone Wild*, the murdered now are not the unfortunate Parisians of Poe's "Murders in the Rue Morgue" but the critically endangered orangutans of Borneo, murdered by human poachers. One woman is murdered by the poachers she has captured on film at the outset of the novel, but it is the orangutan victims who are the focus of the work. Like Peacock's *Melincourt*, Hall's novel is didactic — deliberately crafted to educate its readers about (real) orangutans — their needs, their temperaments, their habitats and the dangers now posed to them by our activities on several fronts. Though Hall's orangutans do not speak or write letters, they offer, like the great apes of *Monkey Planet*, a moral foil to our depredation and destruction.

Gone Wild, like Poe's earlier tale, is in part a detective novel, as the protagonist, Allison Farley — in Borneo to do a count of the remaining orangutans — finds herself instead tracking down her daughter's killers, other poachers and orangutan smugglers. She and her friends also uncover an international plot to create the "last zoo" which involves the murder of scores of endangered species to create the only place where these rare animals can now be seen. Allison and her companions manage to expose this grand plan, and in the course of the novel rescue captive orangutans illegally brought into the United States to stock local private zoos.

The figure of the orangutan as guide and teacher of humans, rather than just critical foil, is still more pronounced in Dale Smith's *What the Orangutan Told Alice* (2004), a novel unashamedly didactic in purpose and tone. It shares with Peacock's *Melincourt* lengthy passages designed to teach readers about orangutans and in this modern case, about their current plight, a plight due entirely to human presence and human practices. Peacock's Sir Oran Haut-ton was a non-speaking example of "natural man", whose presence in the novel implicitly critiqued human urban sophistication, and in case audiences ignored the implications of his behaviour, Sylvan Forester was there to point to the comparison directly. Humans and human societies are also stringently criticised in *What the Orangutan Told Alice*, but the crucial difference is that in this 2004 novel, *humans are held responsible for what they have done to orangutans, other animal species, and the environment;* not for, as in the early nineteenth century novel, their own social inconsistencies and abuses.

The teenage protagonists, Alice and Shane, are visitors to Indonesian Borneo (Kalimantan). Shane is an American exchange student, while Alice has come with her father, who is writing a novel about orangutans. After the two pass into the forest in the company of a male and female gibbon — their passage not so much through as into a "looking glass" that will be held up to them as humans — they meet Anne, a scientist working in orangutan rehabilitation. Alice explains that her father is doing research into orangutans to write "a kind of fantasy thing", a novel:

> "Fantasy? You mean fiction?" Anne's eyebrows arched above her glasses. "Who needs fiction when you've got science?" she said rhetorically.
> "He calls his books 'environmental fiction,'" explained Alice. "He thinks novels are a good way to teach kids about endangered species, you know, like orangutans." (68)

Anne is one of the young adults' two major "teachers" in the novel, and they are receptive listeners. Drawn into the forest by their concern for the gibbons, the apt pupils are led toward their second wise teacher, "the Old Man", by a younger orangutan. It is eventually the Old Man orangutan who shows the children the destruction wrought by humans, while during their journey they learn a great deal about orangutan habits and ways of life.

Though the animals' capacity for speech communication with humans is thus "fantastic", the novel is unremittingly realist in its assessment of species and environmental prospects for an earth dominated by humans and their greed. Marco the orangutan points out to the children the far greater wisdom of the forest dwellers. "Can you name," asks Marco, "another species on this planet who spoils his own home, his own habitat as humans do"? (138). In the forest also, various plants and animals coexist. Enjoining them to look around, their guide points out that there are no landfills, tyre dumps, aluminium cans, Styrofoam cups, or plastic garbage bags. Moreover, "There is no dark cloud of pollution hanging over our heads here. You don't see any animals and plants starving while others are well fed. Here in my world we do not poison our water supplies or make war on each other" (138). The orangutan also shows Shane and Alice the widespread deforestation humans are now causing. Heavy vehicles belching thunderous grey clouds hauled the "mutilated corpses of trees along rutted access roads", while men with red plastic containers dashed the remaining slash piles of limbs and stumps with gasoline. Then there were orange flames and bellowing, energetic masses of rolling smoke. The flames leaped higher and higher and the leaves of trees still standing at the edge of the clear-cut curled against the heat. Everywhere, there was the sound of panic as birds and animals tried to escape. But there was no shelter for the animals ... nowhere for the birds to roost (140).

This destruction is not, however, the end but the beginning of further degradation, caused, as both Anne and the Old Man point out, by human greed, greed that at its most fundamental level is for self-reproduction. What Shane and Alice witness, the old orangutan tells them is "against the laws of nature, but not the laws of men. Man only imagines he has morals, but I could put all the morals man has into my pocket" (140). "As long as human beings keep reproducing at their present rate, it's not going to stop" (141). After the timber is cleared and the slash is burned off, they'll plant rows and rows of oil palms, or rubber trees, or terrace the land for rice paddies. Of course, all the nutrients in the soil will be depleted after two or three years, and after that the crops will fail, and factories and houses will spring up in their places. Towns and villages will grow together to become part of a big bustling city (141).

Anne agrees, and in this novel, neither Westerners nor Indonesians are spared blame. "The problem," she says, "is that there are too many people and they are having way too many babies" (74). Finding humans to have a total lack of respect for the planet, in contrast to other species with whom it should be shared, the Old Man has thought long and hard about human theories of evolution. Since man is emphatically not a part of the natural world, and abuses it so flagrantly, from where did he come? The wise Orangutan concludes that humans are the only species never to have evolved and this is because — the irony of our constant search for extraterrestrials does not escape him — we are in fact aliens ourselves. This, he proposes, is why Cro-Magnon man appears so suddenly (after such a lengthy period of Neanderthal stagnation) and with so many tools; there is in fact no "missing link" between "man" and apes. Indeed, the Old Man is as shocked at the thought of his being genetically related to such a species as were the Victorians at the suggestion they had evolved from apes.

Having passed through a "looking glass" from Indonesian village to forest, then, the two teenagers (unlike Lewis Carroll's Alice) have not really passed into a fantasy world inhabited by strange creatures so much as into a reality check on their own impact on the earth, and in particular on the orangutans and the Borneo rainforest. In spite of its underlying basis in fantasy, the novel employs a quasi-realist mode and includes a great deal of current information on orangutans: the places in which they are most likely to be found, their favourite foods, individual and social behaviours, their dwindling numbers, and the reasons for their accelerating loss of habitat. But it also focuses on the treatment of orangutans by humans, the species responsible for their current condition in what is left of their "wild" and in the variously mean forms of their captivity in Indonesia and other countries.

Melincourt's reviewers criticised Peacock's didacticism and "speechifying", but Smith's novel returns us to didacticism and even to a point of view similar to that of Peacock's philosophical source of inspiration, the Scottish philosopher Monboddo who believed the orangutan to be a branch of mankind, and a superior one at that. When Peacock adopted some of Monboddo's ideas, he did so playfully, only half seriously. Although this novel of the twenty-first century certainly includes light-hearted moments, its attitude toward orangutans (that they are better than humans) is presented just as seriously, if not more so, than in Monboddo's and even Peacock's writings. While Smith's novel obviously employs some anthropomorphic apparatus — the speaking, teaching monkey — it deliberately challenges anthropocentrism and potential dismissals of its own anthropomorphic apparatus by combining its fantasy frame with hard, realist data.

While the two contemporary novels, *Gone Wild*, and *What the Orangutan Told Alice* echo in so many ways, the earlier writing on orangutans, they differ fundamentally from them in their attention to human environmental destruction and human responsibility for the impending loss of the entire orangutan species. Stories of the presence of creatures like orangutans reached Europe in earlier centuries, but for a long time they remained more or less mythological beasts. The tragedy of the twenty-first century may be that the orangutan ceases to exist in the Bornean and Sumatran forests, becoming again — and irrevocably this time — rumour, fantasy, myth and memory.

Works Cited

Boulle, Pierre, *Monkey Planet*, Harmondsworth: Penguin, 1975. Originally published as *La Planete des Singes*, Paris: Julliard, 1963.

Coetzee, John M., *The Lives of Animals*. Princeton NJ, Princeton University Press, 1999.

Cribb, Robert, Helen Gilbert and Helen Tiffin, *Wild Man from Borneo: A Cultural History of the Orangutan*. Honolulu: University of Hawaii Press, 2014.

Hall, James W., *Gone Wild*. New York: Random House, 1996.

Haraway, Donna, *Primate Visions: Gender, Race and Nature in the World of Modern Science*. New York: Routledge, 1989.

Kohler, Wolfgang, *The Mentality of Apes.* New York: Harcourt, Brace, 1926.

Lee, Maurice S., *Slavery, Philosophy and American Literature,* 1830-1860. Cambridge: Cambridge University Press, 2005.

Monboddo, Lord (James Burnet), *Of the Origin and Progress of Language.* London: J. Balfour, 1773.

Peacock, Thomas Love, *Melincourt: Or, Sir Oran Haut-ton.* London, Macmillan 1896 (First edition 1817)

Poe, Edgar Allan, "The Murders in the Rue Morgue". *Graham's Lady's and Gentleman's Magazine,* 18 (1841), 166-179.

Smith, Dale, *What the Orangutan Told Alice.* Nevada City, Calif: Deer Creek Publishing; 2001.

Stowe, Harriet Beecher, *Uncle Tom's Cabin; or, Life Among the Lowly,* 1852.

Woodward, Aylin, "New Species of Orangutan Found". *New Scientist,* 1 November, 2017, p.14.

Chapter 2

Imaginings of Disasters in two Southeast Asian Narratives: Trauma, Risk and Management

Chitra Sankaran,
National University of Singapore, Singapore

Abstract

Despite being a region of the world challenged by a diverse array of first and third-world risk scenarios, Southeast Asia has only gradually come to embrace risk as an intellectual paradigm that may help to allay and manage the threats, dangers and crises that daily beset the populations of diverse nations within ASEAN.

One of the important ways in which trauma and risk are coded, interpreted and managed is through imagining and narrativising disasters. These narratives are moored in history and yet extrapolate to a future that is within the spectrum of plausibility.

In this chapter, I will examine two such narratives from Vietnam and Myanmar that imagine and narrate environmental disaster. Not unsurprisingly, both are firmly rooted in their respective national histories, the former to the Vietnamese War and the use of the toxin popularly referred to as Agent Orange, and the latter negotiating the problems associated with mining in Myanmar.

In examining these narratives, I discuss the scope of risk and its management through an ecocritical reading.

Keywords: Narrative, Risk, Trauma, Myanmar, Vietnam, ecocritical perspectives.

As Donald Trump and Kim Jong-un exchanged tweets about an imminent nuclear attack, our awareness of the escalation of the many risks that surround us in the Anthropocene era was acute. However, the threat of nuclear annihilation appears, sadly, as only one of the manifold risks we face. There is a lot of emphasis on dramatic moments caused by extreme weather or catastrophic human-induced events, but not as much on pedestrian everyday risks and dangers that make up life. In this chapter, I deliberately turn my attention to two narratives that focus not on any apocalyptic moment of risk but on the gradual ways in which risk as fallouts from human acts can erode our everyday lives, depleting it of meaning and filling it with uncertainty and fear. In both texts, the connection between women and animals is stressed, revealing how women as the subdominant gender are made to face risks which, being commonplace, are often invisible. In these narratives, risk and irony appear contiguous.

The discourse of ecofeminism has attempted to bridge the gaps created by both feminists and animal liberationists, whose univocal focus on *either* women's or animal rights issues has failed to identify the common and expansive nature of oppression that connects the two. However, an increasing acknowledgment of the fact that the categories of 'woman' and 'animal' serve the same symbolic function since they are both placed as the submissive 'other' to masculine power, has led to a re-examination of a range of texts that highlight and connect gender concerns with the sorry plight of the non-human. As Lori Gruen remarks, this connection is "not to be understood as a 'natural' connection — one that suggests that women and animals are essentially similar — but rather a constructed connection that has been created by the patriarchy as a means of oppression." (Gruen 61). In the texts I examine, the "non-human" and the "woman" are entangled in interesting ways, and therianthropism — i.e. humans represented as animals — is a strong theme though it is deployed with interesting variations.

The Blood of Leaves

The "Blood of Leaves" by Vietnamese writer Vo Thi Hao explores the implicit assumption that undergirds all patriarchal societies: that women need to be 'ornamental' in order to be useful 'man-servers'. Women who are deemed "ugly" are often accorded 'sub-human' status and equated to animals.

Vo Thi Hao, a graduate of the Faculty of Literature, Hanoi University, worked as an editor of the Ethnic Culture Publishing House. Her publications include both short stories and novels, such as *Salvation Sea, Black Widow and The Pyre*. "The Blood of Leaves" is featured in a collection of Vietnamese short stories entitled *Family of Fallen Leaves,* themed around accounts involving Agent Orange (a herbicide and defoliant), which was sprayed on flora, fauna and people during the Vietnamese war. As the Introduction by Charles Waugh clarifies, the stories by these Vietnamese writers rise from experiences of extreme privation. In the decade between 1961-71, US military sprayed large amounts of chemical defoliants all over Vietnam, in its "jungles, croplands and waterways" (Waugh 1) thus exposing millions, mainly the rural poor and ethnic minorities to the toxic dioxin, a by-product. Even US soldiers and their allies were exposed to this poison which, as Waugh asserts, genetically damaged the soldiers and their progeny, genetically altering them. (Waugh 1).

The entire collection pivots around environmental poisoning and every one of the stories has a character, or characters, deeply affected by or dying due to the effects of the toxic dioxin. Hence, the theme and discourse of risk and also of environmental injustice is centred in this volume. The text as a whole is attentive to the unevenness of global risk. Though several of the stories focus on dramatic events and the risks involved, "The Blood of Leaves" is more restrained. It opens with the first-person narrator meeting up with his friend, Huan, a doctor, who is dying due to Agent Orange. The narrator compares his condition to that of "the yellow leaves of the cycad suffering in its pot next to the bar. It was struggling to grow one small shoot" (134). The local fauna, like humans, has suffered cruelty. The dying Huan gives his friend an assignment: to write love letters to an "ugly" girl, Tam, a midget, possibly born deformed because of the toxic dioxin, who was the sister of Huan's friend, killed in combat.

The oppression of Man over man, woman, and nature that Ariel Salleh observes are "triangulated like a Boromean knot [sic]" (xi) are foregrounded early in the narrative. The cruelty that the "ugly" girl suffers in her daily life is a microcosmic instance of the mass murder committed during the Vietnamese war that is invoked through a graphic image: "A pulse of nausea rose in my throat each time I remembered the knots of green worms writhing in death from Agent Orange. Faced with such human cruelty, each of us was just like those worms", observes the narrator. (Vo 134). The therianthropic representation, as Greg Garrard reminds us "is the reverse of anthropomorphism and is often used in contexts of national or racial stereotyping, such as when Nazis depicted Jews as rats" (141). Humans likened to worms have no more subjectivity than plants and are seen as deserving of destruction.

In this semi-epistolary tale, however, there is an interesting variation. Like Berger's animals (Berger 14), 'ugly' Tam becomes the focus of attention of all the men in the narrative. The narrator reveals that their observations lead to an "ever-extending knowledge" (14) over Tam, who is animalised at many levels. Her life and thoughts become the object of knowledge for three men, the narrator being the last of them. The first, her brother, decides that he needs to generate bogus love letters to assuage her need for love. When shot in the Viet War, he delegates this task to his friend, Huan, who carries on the pretence with the help of the post(wo)man. Finally, the dying Huan requests the narrator to carry on the subterfuge. The story, however, ends on a note that restores Tam's self-respect and agency. When she finds out about the hoax that has been perpetrated on her by three well-meaning men, she refuses their patronage. She establishes her dignity when she quietly declares "Your world is endless but mine is tiny. I have to return to that world." (Vo 146). Her statement though it reveals her vulnerable space reiterates her strength.

Janis Birkeland discusses how the "historic association of women, nature and earth is entrenched in patriarchy. This association automatically relegates nature to the position of a 'man-server'. Both women and nature are valued to the extent that they are useful to Man, underwriting 'instrumentalism' (Birkeland, 1993: 24). The girl in the story is deemed useless despite having an excellent mind, solely on the basis of her physical 'unattractiveness'. When she applies for a place in the university with excellent grades, she is turned down because of her physical appearance.

In fact, the animosity that "ugliness" generates has been well documented in recent years, validating Birkeland's view. Recently, the American, Lizzie Velasquez, born with Marfan syndrome, a rare disease that gives her an aged appearance and makes it hard for the 63lb woman to gain weight, talks about how, when she was 17, someone posted a video of her online and strangers made awful comments, some even telling her to kill herself. Velasquez lived surrounded by risk, threat and even revulsion. But undaunted, she went on to build her life and is today a renowned motivational speaker.[1] Tam's case is similar in the way her "ugly" appearance makes her a target for cruelty, even from her own father and from her close community. Her self-excoriation is revealed in a letter, when she asks, "How did God have the heart to put a good brain inside the head of someone like

---

[1] Her story is available online: http://www.dailymail.co.uk/femail/article-3218362/26-year-old-rare-genetic-disorder-labeled-world-s-ugliest-woman-insists-s-better-thanks-cruel-bullies.html

me, a girl he made by drunken mistake?" (Vo 136-37). The toxins sprayed during the Vietnamese War are the reason for Tam's disfigurement. But she blames her destiny and god rather than history or man. The man-induced risk is made transcendental. As Ulrich Beck observes, risk forms a "shadow kingdom" comparable to the realm of the gods and demons in antiquity, which is hidden behind the visible world and threatens human life on this earth" (Wallace 30).

Tam's death wish, brought on entirely due to her "ugliness" is a telling comment on the instrumental value accorded to women under patriarchy. One of the projects of feminism since its inception has been to write women back into history; women who have been deliberately, purposefully, erased from it. Tam becomes an archetypal example of such a woman. At one point, Huan describes the land withered by war: "The earth all around had turned blackish brown. The trees had completely lost their foliage, leaving the black branches wavering and clutching at everything like ghosts." (Vo 135). The narrative draws implicit comparisons between this dead land and the young girl decimated by the cruelty of the humans around her.

What is enormously courageous and useful about "The Blood of Leaves" is how, in a volume that is focused on the dramatic risks of war induced by Agent Orange, no doubt, a grave and important narrativising of a human-induced "risk" that has had an enduring impact on humans and nature, and about which awareness needs to be raised, Vo manages to sneak in awareness about other, equally harsh risks that so-called 'undesirable women' face, not merely during or through war but as part of their everyday lives. Tam may have been disfigured due to the toxic effects of Agent Orange, but the discrimination and cruelty she faces occur on a daily basis and is suffered to a greater or lesser degree by so-called 'undesirable' women regardless of the circumstances. It is gender-based, given the way beauty and worth are relentlessly linked in women the world over. The narrator's insightful statement "The street bubbled with hostility ...War's not the only place to find it" (Vo 144) reveals her intention to expose the risks and cruelty women are routinely subjected to. For the so-called ugly girls like Tam and Lizzie, the social world becomes a field of war, and their everyday lives an ongoing battle. The "rhetoric of animality" is as functional in descriptions of human social and political relations as it is in describing actual animals. (Steve Baker, Cited in Garrard 140).

Heartless Forest

The second text is an interesting titular story from "Heartless Forest" (2013) about forest fire by Myanmarese writer Khin Mya Zin. In 2012, her short story collection *Clouds in the Sky and Other Stories* won the

Myanmar National Literary Award. *The Heartless Forest: An Anthology of Burmese Women Writers* was edited by Mon Mon Myat and Nancy Cunningham. The narrative once again pivots around risk, here the danger of forest fires, but it is calm, even tranquil, in tone and in the mood it sets. In a lyrical, strangely haunting tale, we discover about Nyein, who is dead and roams the forests as a spirit following the movements of her husband, who is alive and unconscious of her presence, in contrast to the animals, who sense her ghostly form. The story invokes a connection between the human, the spirit and the animal worlds sketching an animistic vision of earth. The narrative can be seen to unfold within the tradition of Myanmarese classical poetry. In a lecture delivered by Lé Lé Wynn from the University of Yangon during the Irrawaddy Literary Festival, Wynn discusses the different genres that present their close affinity to Nature:

> *tawlar-ratus* (တောလားရတု) and seasonal verses (ရာသီဖွဲ့) such as *moetaw-ratu* (မိုးတောရတု), *moephwé* (မိုးဖွဲ့), *nwayphwé* (နွေးဖွဲ့), and so forth are the best examples to understand that the Myanmar (sic) feel a close affinity with Nature and that they appreciate the beauties of Nature and its seasonal changes. (3)

Wynn explains that the term "tawlar" literally translates to "a journey through the forest". These romantic expressions about Nature date back to the fourteenth century (3).

As in the *tawlar-ratu*, here the spirit Nyein roams through the forest delighting in its many sights and sounds. The unusually lyrical language and poetic passages could show a direct link to this tradition. Also, true to the spirit of *tawlar-ratu*, the human spirit is not separated from the plants and animals. Furthermore, Nyein's embedment in nature as a spirit means that she is as much the observed as the observer. Invisible to her husband, she is constantly watched by the animals. The unusual narrative thus contravenes Garrard's view, largely true though West-centric, that in human discourse animals are always the observed.

The fact that they can observe us has lost all significance. They are the objects of our ever-extending knowledge. What we know about them is an index of our power, and thus an index of what separates us from them. The more we know, the further away they are. (Garrard 139; Berger 14).

In "Heartless Forest", the idea of observation is central, but the gaze is not human. The dead Nyein stalks her husband, enters his dreams at will, and wanders inside his hut in the middle of the forest. Also, the animals — the domesticated dog and the wild panther — stalk Nyein and keep her under surveillance. The animals sense her presence but the man doesn't. The man's obliviousness is contrasted to the animals' perception:

> Dogs are not like him
> They have sharp eyes and ears.
> They seem to know that she is there.
> They would get up to bark and howl in the dark of the night (Khin 48)

The act of seeing is posited as a primordial activity, preceding words. As Berger points out, "It is seeing which establishes our place in the surrounding world." (*Ways of Seeing* 1). What is interesting is that in the surveillance is the watchfulness that accompanies anxieties about risk. Clearly, all parties involved assume danger from the other and are vigilant in order to safeguard themselves. Ironically, only the human male appears supremely unaware of this unfolding tension that surrounds him. This is a telling and sardonic comment on the exploitative human male largely oblivious to the impact of his actions on the surrounding environment.

Like liberationist critics, Khin appears to want to undermine the moral and legal distinctions between humans and animals. Though her humanness and her capacity for emotion are conveyed, as a spirit being, Nyein appears closer to the flora and fauna than to her husband from whom she was distanced even while alive. When Nyein comes across her husband, in his "worn-out blue jeans and his old brown coat" (41), we are told that though Nyein does not try to go up to him, he focuses on the space she stands in. However, the dog appears to sense her spirit presence. In a significant insistence on the act of gazing, we are told,

> He walks towards the tree where Nyein is.
> He stands under the tree.
> In the thick darkness, leaning against the strong tree trunk, Nyein stares at him.
> (p.42)

Hence, scrutiny, a primal activity, is allied to risk and danger. The man "fixes his eyes" on where Nyein's spirit-being stands, while the dog "barks as though she has seen Nyein"; "Nyein "stares" at her husband (42-3). At other times "Nyein has followed the panther, spying on it, but it slipped away into a thicket. Before disappearing, it looked at where Nyein was with its piercing eyes" (43). The circle is now complete, setting up a connective link through these acts of surveillance, a network and a reciprocity between humans, the spirit and animals. This *quid pro quo* inspection deliberately undermines the hierarchy that Erica Fudge points out is established by the always one-sided human observation of animals. (*Perceiving Animals* 4).

The ecocritic's sustained interest in the subjectivity of the non-human and in the problems of the troubled boundaries between the human and other creatures (Garrard 148) is also echoed in the narrative. Interestingly though, the binary that's usually drawn between domestic and wild animals along gendered lines with the domestic constructed as female and the latter, male, common across wilderness narratives that Barney Nelson discusses (*The Wild and the Domestic: Animal Representation, Ecocriticism, and Western American Literature*) does not get duplicated here. On the contrary, the domesticated dog and the wild panther appear almost interchangeable in the narrative.

> Nyein looks to see if the animal moving among the crops is the panther.
> It is his dog.
> The dog, looking at the milkwood tree, howls long and loud (44)

Here, panther and dog appear interchangeable and kindred. It is the man who stands apart. Nyein's animosity toward her husband plays out the classic pattern of man against woman and nature. While she was alive, "Nyein's favourite dog was killed in the snare set up to catch the boar. He did not see that Nyein was desperate from that time on" (44). When alive "[o]n a page of the book, Nyein wrote with her small handwriting, "I hate him most of all" (44). Nyein's estrangement from her husband also signals the distance between the man and the natural world of which Nyein seems a part. Descriptions of her ease and embedment in nature abound: "She hid in the dark bamboo clumps all day. Sometimes, bamboo-cutters came, and then Nyein jumped from top of one bamboo cane to another" (47). Yet, the narrative also disrupts such neat binaries, for, when the man marries Nyein, his first request to her is "Will you love my woods like I do, Nyein?" (42). Back then "Nyein was afraid of the sound of forest... the forest was no pleasant place for Nyein. It was terrifying" (45). But her fear is also because she appears more closely attuned to dimensions he appears unaware of, since he is shown as merely residing in the forest, relating to it only at a superficial level, whereas she is alert to its every nuance. At night, Nyein heard the wind whisper. To her it was the spirits talking. The shaking branches become ghostly hands who might catch her. But the man is impervious to this subtle world. She wonders "Why did he not see these things?" (45)

The man's obtuseness is a cause of their estrangement, as also their differing attitudes to animals and the land that killed Nyein in the first place.

While his tending of the forest and land are pragmatic and functional, hers are born out of love. He sets up traps to kill animals that destroy his fields, to safeguard his crops. She cannot accept this. The divide is categorical:

Rabbits would dig up the radishes. Deer would trample the bean fields, and devour the beans. The sparrows and drongos that Nyein loved stripped the whole sesame crop.

> Nyein did not like the killing of animals.
> They did not speak to each other (46)

From then on, their relationship is in a downward spiral. Nyein catches a fever and is left uncared for. After her recovery, she retreats into herself and only talks to her dead dog. But the man is unfeeling:

> He thought she was just play-acting.
> He gave her stern looks. She responded to his glares with fear. She vanished from the cabin.
> Nyein's body was found down by the stream, at the water's edge. (46)

The man's unsympathetic, utilitarian attitude towards nature and animals is in sharp contrast to the symbiosis Nyein seeks and finds in the biotic forest community, even more after her death. On another level, it is significant that it is his "stern looks" that wilts her for she responds to them "with fear" and subsequently "vanished from the cabin" (46). Indeed, even when she dies and ceases to be part of this community, as a ghost she appears to be harmonised with nature almost as though she were embodied. "On moonless nights, Nyein walked throughout the forest.... On such nights, she would drive away the wild dogs that stalked the sweet rabbits...." (47). She embeds herself in Nature "sometimes coiling on the ground like a boa constrictor", and at others, when she heard the sound of woodpeckers, "She would ... guard the baby birds in their nests." (48).

Though Nyein seamlessly blends in with nature, she is presented as in part embedded in culture too, because, "[s]ome nights, Nyein hid between the pages of her book of poems. She would play with the words moving them around. For example, she would move the word *hate* from here to there." (48) Hence, the narrative blurs the divide that generates a gendered view of the nature/culture divide. The ending of this lyrical narrative is brought about by another elemental force, a forest fire. Nyein catches the smell of fire and sees the animals hurtling away. "The panther looks long at Nyeine" (48) before dashing headlong into the forest. Nyein runs to the man's cabin but finds that the "fire swallows the hut" (49). Nyein searching in vain but cannot locate the man: "Where is he? ... The woods he loves escapes the fire... The fire passes on, leaving only ashes and coals." (50) The following passage bespeaks calm after the ravages of the fire but also fulfils a pattern while signalling a beginning.

> There is a crescent moon.
> A shadow moves under a tree.
> It's the panther.
> The panther watches Nyein.
> When she approaches him, he does not turn away as before.
> In the dark, the panther's eye glint green
> The green eyes sparkle like electric bulbs in the darkness of night.
> (50)

The idea of observation — watching and being watched that initiated the narrative — also concludes it. Like the *tawlar*-ratu, the journey through the forest is fulfilled by the act of seeing, hence bonding fauna, flora and female spirit.

Concluding thoughts

Both texts in this chapter make critical connections between women and animals, expanding on the ecofeminist discourse around interconnectedness, speciesism, empathy, risk, violence and trauma. They passionately narrativise against the pervasive speciesism of humans. Their narratives draw nuanced connections between sexism and speciesism, and, in the process, foreground many underlying causes of the modern environmental crisis such as chauvinism and human disconnection from the animal world. They stand testimony to the observation by Ulrich Beck that risk society does not emerge suddenly and dramatically "In the manner predicted in the picture books of social theory; rather the transition occurs on the tiptoes of normality, via the backstairs of side-effects." (*Risk Society* 11).

Works Cited

Beck, Ulrich. *Risk Society: Towards a New Modernity*. Trans. Mark Ritter. London: Sage Publications, 1992.

Berger, John. "Why Look at Animals?" Berger, John. *About Looking*. New York: Vintage, 1980. 3-30.

Birkeland, Janis. "Ecofeminism: Linking Theory and Practice." *Ecofeminism*. Ed. Greta Gaard. Philadelphia: Temple University Press, 1993.

Fudge, Erica. *Perceiving Animals*. New York: Palgrave Macmillan, 2000.

Garrard, Greg. *Ecocriticism*. The New Critical Idiom Series. London & New York: Routledge, 2004.

Gruen, Lori. "Dismantling Oppression: An Analysis of the Connection between Women and Animals." *Ecofeminism: Women, Animals, Nature*. Ed. Greta Gaard. Philadelphia: Temple University Press, 1993. 60-89.

Khin, Mya Zin. "Heartless Forest." *Heartless Forest: An Anthology of Burmese Women Writers*. Ed. Nance Cunningham and Mon Mon Myat. Yangon, Myanmar: Pangodan Books, 2013. 41-50.

Nelson, Barney. *The Wild and the Domestic: Animal Representation, Ecocriticism and Western American Literature*. Reno and Las Vegas: University of Nevada Press, 2000.

Salleh, Ariel. *Ecofeminism as Politics: Nature, Marx and the Postmodern*. London: Zed Books and New York: St Martins Press.1997.

Vo, Thi Hao. "The Blood of Leaves." *Family of Fallen Leaves: Stories of Agent Orange by Vietnamese Writers*. Ed. Charles Waugh and Lien Huy. Athens, Georgia and London: University of Georgia Press, 2010. 134-46.

Wallace, Molly. *Risk Criticism: Precautionary Reading in an Age of Environmental Uncertainty*, Ann Arbor, Michigan: University of Michigan Press, 2016.

Waugh, Charles. "Introduction." *Family of Fallen Leaves: Stories of Agent Orange by Vietnamese Writers*. Ed. Charles and Huy, Lien Waugh. Athens, Georgia and London: University of Georgia Press, 2010. 1-16.

Wynn, Le Le. "The Role of Myanmar Poems in Environmental Conservation." *Irrawaddy Literary Festival*. 3 2 2013.

Chapter 3

Georgic Gastronomies: Restorative Eating in the Anthropocene with Margaret Atwood and Merlinda Bobis

Jose Monfred C. Sy,
University of the Philippines, Philippines

Abstract

Nobel Laureate Paul Crutzen and chemist Eugene Stoermer pronounce that the planet has entered the Anthropocene, a geologic time where humans have become the primary agents of environmental change in more palpable ways. This era is characterised by the food-related, political economic, and ecological crises we face today. For instance, in recent decades, agro-transnational corporations have been aggressively co-opting small-scale and local agricultural networks into a system that dislocates food producers from consumers. Such operations account for 85% of consumptive water use, deforestation projects, significant losses in biodiversity, and a third of manmade greenhouse gas emissions. Food, so to speak, is a major driver of environmental change. In forming counternarratives against neoliberal geopolitics, we must first create environmentally conscious publics. Thus, the humanities are challenged to find ways of representing and reimagining the principles that buttress the Anthropocene. Responding to this call, I offer Margaret Atwood's *Oryx and Crake* and *The Year of the Flood* and Merlinda Bobis' *Locust Girl: A Lovesong* as novels that foreground the often-ignored nexus among food justice, human inequality, and ecological crises in the Anthropocene, restoring readers to a sense of self and place in our troubled biosphere. Through the pastoral momentum of retreat-and-return, the survivors of these narratives destabilise the perverted conception of food in our era. By subjecting both human and non-human entities to the same rules of exploitation and consumption, these novels restore to readers a sense of ecological community in a troubled biosphere.

Keywords: post-pastoral; ecotopian fiction; food crisis; environmental justice; companion species; scale-crossing environmentalism.

> The mind, that ocean where each kind
> Does straight its own resemblance find;
> Yet it creates, transcending these,
> Far other worlds, and other seas;
> Annihilating all that's made
> To a green thought in a green shade.
> — Andrew Marvell, "The Garden" (1681)

Crises in Context

An integrating and uneven global food enterprise is colonising matters of local food security. In a report on food security presented to the 16th Congress of the Philippines, biotechnologist Harvey Glick contended that current practices in Philippine agriculture could not quash threats of a nationwide food shortage, and to him, the local government must implement sound food security policies that encourage the use of modern agricultural biotechnology (Romero "Expert warns"). Interestingly, Dr. Glick serves as a senior expert for Monsanto, which stands among the most profitable transnational companies (TNC's) in the world, with revenues representing an estimated 90% of the Genetically Modified Organisms (GMO) market (Carruth 15). We cannot help but wonder if Glick's proposal, which spells severe repercussions for small-scale farmers and the rural poor, only seeks to solidify US agrodominance and advance a neoliberal food regime[1] (Sommerville et al. 256). Corporate sourcing strategies have been co-opting agriculture as but a paltry component, severing it from traditions surrounding harvest, preparation and mealtimes (Weis 16). Adversely, despite tremendous gains in global agricultural productivity, nearly a billion people remain hungry (Carruth 4). In contemporary geopolitics, this food crisis is widely understood (and represented) as a symptom of a world in need of greater economic integration through neoliberal policies where "market openness and economic interdependence and connectivity are

---

[1] In agrarian systems such as the Philippine *hacienda*s, exorbitantly priced biotechnological products are forcibly loaned to poor farmers by landlords under the pretext of upgrading traditional practices. While this means profit for TNC's such as Monsanto, it only compounds the financial burden levied upon farmers and rural communities.

enthusiastically embraced [...] for advancing food security" (Sommerville et al. 243). This enterprise sows the myth of a highly productive "North" that can rescue an impoverished "South" from the food crisis, as seen in the case of the Philippines.

Further complicating this is the dependence of food industries on the biosphere. Covering about 40% of the planet's landmass, agricultural operations account for 85% of consumptive water use, deforestation projects, significant losses in biodiversity, and a third of manmade greenhouse gas emissions (Sommerville et al. 254). Food, so to speak, is also a major driver of environmental change. Looking at it from the bigger picture, everything we eat is intricately linked to scale-crossing crises ranging from the ecological (climate change, land degradation, widespread pollution) to the socio-political (farmers and workers' exploitation, land dispossession, community displacement).

Activist Bill McKibben asks, "we can register what is happening with satellites and scientific instruments, but can we register it in our imaginations, the most sensitive of all our devices?" ("What the Warming World") Despite the traction environmental activism has gained in recent decades,[2] the contingencies of food, politics, and ecology remain tenuous, if not invisible, to the public. Ecocritic Hillary Sullivan, for instance, scorns how "we revel in (dwindling) lush landscapes while traveling the globe and seeking ever 'better' energy practices; [adversely,] we race towards ever faster resource extraction and energy use, while the slow violence of pollution, massive extinction rates, melting ice caps, wild storms, and the warming climate all fade away in the face of lunch choices" (57). This reality may be a bitter pill to swallow, but such are the material conditions in the Anthropocene, the era when human impacts have shaped geologic time (Crutzen & Stoermer 17). The impact is characterised not only by environmental ills but also by the upswing in capitalism and the spread of industrial particulates over the entire globe, forces that further dilate the exploitation of natural resources (Sullivan 47). Hunger-amidst-abundance now shapes global politics (Sommerville et al. 242, Weis 12). Denigrating our species for such a denial would discount the difficulty of showing the link between one's breakfast and the Anthropogenic catastrophe taking

---

[2] In the 1960's, environmental activism began to garner much following in the U.S. after the publication of Rachel Carson's *Silent Spring*, a famous exposé that documents the pernicious effects of agribusiness activities, particularly those of Monsanto.

place outside the kitchen.[3] To respond to the swelling violence of the era, partially driven by food production and consumption, we must develop a means to *imagine* the scale and impact of human eating activity, and in this study, I propose that we direct our attention to the novel.

Literature, I believe, is an instrument attuned to the modern food system due to its tendency to shuttle between intimate (the dining table) and interpersonal (the food industry) registers. To demonstrate this capability, I turn to the works of two writers, Margaret Atwood and Merlinda Bobis. Atwood's *Oryx and Crake* (2003) and its sequel *The Year of the Flood* (2009), and Bobis' most recent novel, *Locust Girl: A Lovesong* (2015), lodge their critique of the Anthropocene through *eco*topian fiction, an increasingly popular contemporary cultural form well-suited to imagining food geopolitics[4] (Vials 237). I choose to put Atwood, a Canadian, and Bobis, a Filipina-Australian, in dialogue because they cultivate a scale-crossing environmental consciousness that straddles across national borders, refracting the globe-trotting tendencies of agro-industrial TNC's.[5] Like how the discourse of food shuffles between local and global contexts, these novels imagine the haywire contingencies of food, politics, and ecology by vacillating between macroscopic and intimate scales of representation. The surprisingly pastoral flourish of these texts represents the Anthropocene finally *aware* of itself, through which they offer not only an exposé of but also potential remedies to the crises of the era. Ultimately, these works of fiction subject both human and non-human entities to the same rules of exploitation and consumption, restoring readers to a sense of ecological community in a troubled biosphere. Because of a rootedness in the lived experience of the Anthropocene, their novels make the reader aware of the neoliberal enterprise and geopolitics that remain tenuous in an era where food production and consumption take place separately.

---

[3] The spaces of food production and consumption are separated by globalization, which relies on the exportation and importation of resources, labor, and goods. This intensifies the phenomenon Karl Marx called "commodity fetishism." To put it simply, the meals served on our tables are severed from the material conditions that generate them.

[4] In this study, food shall be understood not only a basic human necessity; it is also "a system of communication with the capacity to create meaning beyond its materiality" (Caruth 9). To invoke Roland Barthes, food in contemporary society is "polysemic"—it bears multiple social and ecological meanings that shape its materiality (33-34).

[5] Of course, I also wish to introduce to a wider audience a Philippine novel in English, although, as already pointed out and shall be explained further, *Locust Girl*'s mythos is scale-crossing.

Hungry Hearts

(Post-)Anthropocenes. Winner of the prestigious Christina Stead Prize for Fiction, *Locust Girl: A Lovesong* is Merlinda Bobis' fourth novel. It provides readers with the coming-of-age story of Amedea, the eponymous Locust Girl, who gets buried deep in the sands of a desert-like wasteland after her village's destruction (Bobis 8). A locust "nibbled its way under [her] forehead and there [she] slept [her] ten-year sleep" (9). Unlike Bobis' other works,[6] *Locust Girl* is pure fantasy, leaving any pretense of realism behind to essay her message more clearly (Sussex "*Locust Girl*").

The world order in Bobis' world echoes an anxiety towards agrodominance. After she awakens from her sleep, Amedea travels across a border that demarcates the wasteland and the lush country called the Five Kingdoms. People who do not possess the capacity to conserve the environment, the wasters, are withheld outside the border, within which live the paranoid and privileged carers with their abundance of food. In Bobis' Anthropocene, body parts are traded, (71) color-coded radios spiel the ruling party's propaganda, (7-8) and the border is fiercely defended using fire, which by that time is also a scarce resource (140). A character Amedea meets, Grandfather Opi, recites the event that has jettisoned the accruing crises of the Anthropocene into a climax:

> But each of the countries secretly wished to control all grains and seeds, all waters and animals, all oils, all colours, even all dreams, so they fought each other with great fires ... So the biggest countries embraced each other to become the biggest and strongest country with the greatest fire. (103-4)

Such a world order is an upshot of the same global enterprise introduced earlier, which scours for "new markets [...] raw materials, goods and labour" across the world, contributing to a loss of rights over nature for the sake of the expansion of capital and generation of profit (Loomba 256, 258). Underneath Amedea's lyrical bildungsroman is a pointed political allegory.

A sharp relief to Bobis' poetic language, Margaret Atwood employs a political vocabulary more familiar to the mainstream audience (Vials 241). Now part of the acclaimed MaddAddam trilogy with *The Year of the Flood*

---

[6] These include *Banana Heart Summer*, *The Solemn Lantern Maker*, and *Fish-Hair Woman*. All of which insinuate the supernatural in the mundane "real" world, unlike the fantastical *Locust Girl*.

and *MaddAddam* (2013), *Oryx and Crake* was first published on the 50th anniversary of the discovery of the structure of DNA and in the same year that the entire human genome was sequenced. Atwood's two novels imagine the possible consequences of such stages of scientific enlightenment, which at this point are an issue but not yet a fact that can be observed and measured (McKibben[b] 183). They are responses to the accelerating pollution in North America, (Howells 161) what the author herself considers as "definitive moments," after which "things were never the same again" (Atwood[b] 4).

Oryx and Crake and *The Year of the Flood* are lacerated by fragments of the past, through which we learn that capitalism has achieved "its authoritarian ends [...] using [a neoliberalist] narrative means which has emerged over the last 25 years" (Vials 237). The capitalist market has won, and class inequality is clear and absolute: the privileged few reside in gated communities called 'the Compounds,' akin to modern day company towns, while everyone else lives in desperate, crime-ridden urban areas referred to as 'the pleeblands'. *Oryx and Crake* focuses on the Compound life and survival exploit of Jimmy (also known as Snowman), while *The Year of the Flood*, to pose an alternative, shifts its focus to the lives and beliefs of God's Gardeners, particularly the beekeeper Toby and young Ren. This faction braids revolutionary science and religion, "holding all life sacred, use only recycled items, and insist on leaving as small an imprint on the Earth as humanly possible" (Pressley 115). The high-tech world in the two novels has been damned by Crake's megalomaniac bioterrorism project, what the Gardeners Toby and Ren call the Waterless Flood, and Jimmy the Great Rearrangement. The plague unleashed by Crake is encapsulated by the Paradice Project's BlyssPluss Pill. The Pill marketed all over the world by Jimmy, Oryx (Crake's love interest), and some members of a "MaddAddam" resistance group—"gave you the best sex ever, but it had serious side effects, such as death [...] That's how the pandemic plague got started" (Atwood[c] 395). Jimmy, Toby, and Ren recall Crake's calamity as they navigate through the post-Anthropocene.

Atwood and Bobis' novels demand critical attention as they render our contested era visible. In contrast to the more well-known utopian and dystopian strains, the materialist ecotopia uses pressing eco-political issues as a lens in coloring its alternative world (Cotgrove 23).[7] These

---

[7] The ecotopian acknowledgement that a "utopia" cannot be utopian to all its inhabitants tailors the three novels to the task of representing our era where utopian obesity and dystopian famine can coexist. Parallels in theme and scale between the

visions function as narrative machines that challenge our approach to our present situation (Moylan *xi*). Instead of comparing their dystopian presents with an idyllic "greener" past that can serve as a model for remedying the current crises, these novels shift among events occurring immediately before and after an "apocalyptic" upshot.

Amedea, Jimmy, Toby, and Ren's declension to the past is dramatised as an act of border crossing, a political activity motivated by none other than hunger. Here, the contingencies of food, politics, and ecology are rendered visible. Throughout literary history, the materiality of the border warrants a disruption of human and ecological communities (Fiskio 136). Such a border is central to a world order as clear-cut as Bobis'. The Five Kingdoms are governed by the Honorable Head Zacarem with the aid of the Ministers of Legs, Mouths, and Arms. They explain to Amedea that the border preserves what is left of the Earth's natural sources as it keeps out wasters (Bobis 164). The Five Kingdoms' monopoly over the last remaining natural resources in the planet solidifies their power over the rest of humanity, whose survival depends on food.

In the Anthropocene of *Oryx and Crake* and *The Year of the Flood*, the borders facilitating the transactions between the bourgeois-like Compounds and the decaying pleeblands are maintained not by a state government like Five Kingdoms, but by the CorpSeCorps, which "were running the army, now that it had been privatized" (Atwood[c] 266). The market and the laws protecting it "[are] enforced entirely by the CorpSeCorps, which began as a private security firm, but gradually developed into a functional equivalent of a state" (Vials 241). Soon, "the CorpSeCorps were sending their tentacles everywhere" (Atwood[c] 25). The nation-state has been dissolved to make way for a self-regulating market— indeed, a capitalist utopia, including its services such as the police force. Parallel to the Five Kingdoms, Compounds such as HelthWyzer, OrganInc Farms, and NooSkins, each named after a pharmaceutical or bio-engineering firm, hold a monopoly over food production and storage. As the Kingdoms preserve the last of natural resources, the Compounds have the luxury to use science to develop synthetic food despite the "disease" that keeps on spreading (Atwood[a] 18-9). The Five Kingdoms address a similar anxiety towards the depletion of their natural resources not only through the border but also using the radio-like orange boxes that instruct wasters of their territory (Bobis 10) and the "forgetting seeds" that erase

---

genre and the Anthropocene (like this and those mentioned in the essay) make science fiction novels exciting platforms for theorizing our era.

their memories for good (157). These measures that bolster the effectivity of the border are telling of the elite's fear against potential dissenters (Bobis 164).

Cannibalism in the Anthropocene. The border that facilitates food production and consumption produces a dual system of political subjects. First, there are those who populate the center of agrodominance and biotechnology. Represented by the carers, Jimmy, Crake and the citizens of the Compounds, they enjoy a democratic order that affords liberal rights of property. Adversely, the principle of exclusive property continually necessitates what social philosopher Giorgio Agamben calls the *state of exclusion* — zones such as the plantation, the colony, the ghetto, wherein human beings exist as *Homines sacri*, or bare life (qtd. in Kershaw 274). These non-subjects, represented in the novels by the wasters and the pleeblanders, are "stripped of every right and living under a palpable threat of death" (Agamben qtd. in Vials 243-4). Being at the core of the narrative at hand, Amedea, Toby, and Ren speak for the pool of under- and unemployed surplus of humanity that inhabit the state of exception.

In Atwood and Bobis' frightening ecotopian visions, political exclusion is not the direst encumbrance in the state of exception. Already deprived of food, the wasters and pleeblanders become natural resources themselves, ripe for extraction. The smell of meat reeks from the Five Kingdoms as they cook both animals and the condemned bodies of dissenters (Bobis 162). In the pleeblands, seeing human meat on the SecretBugers grill is no surprise. "The secret of SecretBurgers was that no one knew what sort of animal protein was actually in them [...] Was there a human fingernail, once? It was possible. The local pleebmobs paid the CorpSeCorpsMen to turn a blind eye" (Atwood[c] 33). Even in problems such as burying the dead Pilar, the God's Gardeners' resident mycologist, Toby could not "just leave her in a vacant lot for the scavengers, [because] she might end up in a SecretBurger" (185). With the scarcity of food, people have been less picky about their animal protein.

Bare life cannibalism takes place not only physically, but also emblematically. The scant rations in Bobis' Anthropocene, which usually include seeds, oils, and waters, are not given for free because "rewards must be equally shared [...] Rewards were harvested under the blanket. Eyes here, last good leg there, maybe that hand with the ring. And deeper down, more precious parts that could be traded across the border" with "the men scavenging for a heart, a liver, a kidney" (80). The wasteland serves as human farms to the Five Kingdoms, which harvest body parts and even comfort women called "green trees" whenever they see fit. "*What is yours* [the wasters'] *will be ours*," the carers sing proudly. As one of the wasters yelled, "what's more criminal than selling to us what's rightfully ours?" (72) In *Oryx and Crake* and *The Year of the Flood*, the same occurs in the occasion of the pigoon. "The goal of the pigoon project was to grow an assortment of foolproof human-tissue organs in a transgenic knockout pig host [...] Such a host animal could be reaped of its extra kidneys" (Atwood[a] 22-3). Animals are exploited to serve human infirmities. Despite the medical intent of this project, we see pigoons served on the table: "Pigoon pie again [...] Pigoon pancakes, pigoon popcorn," Jimmy used to complain (Atwood[a] 24). In a world of ultra-advanced biotechnology, human parts can be confused for animal ones and even eaten.[8]

By positioning humans as objects of consumption, they trace back scarcity to the perverted conception of food in our Anthropocene. To Crake and the artist companions of Jimmy, "it had been game over once agriculture was invented, six or seven thousand years ago. After that, the human experiment was doomed, first to gigantism due to a maxed-out food supply, and then to extinction" (Atwood[a] 243). Agricultural practice, which now is an agro-imperial enterprise, is excessively levying a toxic burden to the biosphere and is driving the epochal environmental crises of biodiversity loss and climate change (Weis 5, 10). Cho-Choli, a mentor to Amedea, tearfully relates that long ago, "good men and women" have pilfered their water source in order to redistribute it more equitably. They have received no such water, however, drying up the village and the "wombs of [their] women" (Bobis 42). Like Grandfather Opi, Cho-Choli traces back scarcity to an imperialistic project that monopolises certain markets, such as water. These anthropogenic operations that exploit the physical environment revolve around the accumulation of food for human beings. As such, their justification for the existence of the non-human aspects of nature is utility (93). In this perspective, food motivates ecological crises because of its utility to our species, the primary shaper of nature in the Anthropocene. Atwood and Bobis develop a world where the attitude that led to panoramic scarcity endures. If the Anthropocene concept of "food" refers to nothing but a natural resource to be exploited and consumed, then count that humans dispossessed of food—now the currency of political exchange—are on the menu.

---

[8] There are other gene splice experiments in *Oryx and Crake* and *The Year of the Flood*, such as the ChickieNobs, which blur the difference between humans, animals, and consumable food. However, only pigoons have evolved to possess superior, human-level intellect.

The epistemological basis of the above antagonism, signified and exacerbated by the border, is none other than food. Economic interchange, that is, the distribution of goods, must be facilitated by a border that can ensure the preservation of edible natural resources. However, this remedy to a global crisis is too utopian an ideal. Policymaking around the question "who gets what" in order to control consumption rates only consigns the unlucky many to poverty, to not getting any *at all*. By reifying the paradox of hunger and abundance in the Anthropocene, the novels facilitate a politics of seeing that expands plain recognition "by foregrounding the lives and experiences of those *hardest hit* by ecological injustice and those with the *least responsibility* for the problems," vis-à-vis ecological disaster (Sze 104). More interestingly, by dramatising how Anthropogenic conditions subject both human and non-human entities to the same rules of exploitation and consumption, the novels radically disturb our unruffled perception of food, calling out attention to the complicated ecological geopolitics obscured in the process of eating one's meal.

Pastoral Perceptions

Taken as gastronomies — writings that correlate food and culture, *Locust Girl*, *Oryx and Crake*, and *The Year of the Flood* expose what eating in the Anthropocene is: a monstrous activity which fetishises the simultaneous exploitation of the natural environment and other human beings. They all smack of *georgic* art, which depicts how utility dominates over pastoral care (Gifford 23). The implementation of extractive neoliberal policies in response to the food crisis, which seek to close the 'yield gap' between a 'highly productive' North and an 'under-producing' South, (258) are rendered complete in *Locust Girl*, *Oryx and Crake*, and *The Year of the Flood*. This culmination turns "all human beings and physical landscapes into pure commodities, annihilating the natural environment and the very basis of human society" (Vials 236). Historically speaking, proponents of neoliberalist policies succeed in convincing publics that this chaos can be solved by yet more neoliberalism (240). As food security increasingly becomes an urgent issue central to discussions of national, ecological, and human security, climate change, and global inequality (Sommerville et. al. 240) a counter-geopolitics perspective must attend to governmental efforts in countering aggressively productive food systems and its safeguards, such as "the installation of 'selectively permeable' borders that reproduce the global North as a zone of relatively greater food security and privilege compared to the South" (253-4).

Wishing to heed this call, I close this essay by arguing that Atwood and Bobis' novels can be interpreted beyond their potency in rendering visible the contingencies of food, politics, and ecology. Having read the novels in meaningful dialogue with the food crisis facilitated by the North-South antagonism, we can outsource from them potential remedies to the neoliberal imagination that buttresses the Anthropocene. By imperiling humans and what we would now consider edible nonhuman species to the same forms of exploitation and consumption, the novels remind readers that we are all part of a single ecological community beleaguered by Anthropogenic destruction. As Atwood and Bobis extend our era's perverse epistemology of food to futuristic ecotopian visions, they also intimate us to protagonists who destabilise such a destructive perception by demonstrating an ethics stemming from a sense of ecological community. Amedea, Jimmy, Toby, and Ren realise this through the pastoral momentum of retreat-and-return. The concept of the pastoral, which traditionally contrasts rurality and urbanity, (Sullivan 48) is helpful in a discussion of humanity's relation to the natural environment (Evernden 99). Pastoralist Terry Gifford explains that the pastoral formulae evoke two opposing sentiments: "the deeply green ecological ideals still at the core of much ecocriticism and environmentalism, yet also a darkly tainted history of imperialistic power struggles both local and global over land use" (qtd. in Sullivan 48). This double preoccupation is embraced by Gifford's concept of the post-pastoral. It is not so much a description of a genre as it is a formula for extracting the texts' wiles on humanity vis-à-vis naturality (47-8). The ecocritical trope is best used to delineate works that suggest a collapse between the human/nature divide while being aware of the complications involved (Gifford 26). It reaches beyond the limitations of the traditional pastoral while being recognisably within the tradition, and thus it can refer to a work of any period.

The post-pastoral orchestrates its mutual interrogation of humanity and naturality by the momentum of retreat and return—return, in the broadest sense of the word (19). This could mean a return to humanity as in the famous *Walden* by Henry David Thoreau, or, as I shall suggest in this paper, a *restoration*. The protagonists in Atwood and Bobis' novels perform the pastoral momentum by the very act of border-crossing. If a perverted epistemology of food motivates the establishment of the border, then the same would invite resistance. As proclaimed by Adam One, "hunger is a powerful reorganizer of conscience" (Atwood[c] 33). For the Five Kingdoms, hunger is a non-issue: "We can address hunger [...] We have mechanisms for consumption and control. Hunger is a non-word now" (164). In reply, Amedea persists that hunger has motivated her movement to the Kingdoms. She even snaps, "what do we deserve? [...] What if we're hungry?" (151) The wasteland as a state of exception is ripe for dissent.

In *Oryx and Crake*, hunger motivates Jimmy to cross the borders of the post-plague world. After much consideration, he decides to "prioritize. Whittle things down to essentials. The essentials are: *Unless you eat, you die* (Atwood[a] 152). In order to secure food, he sets out for the RejoovenEsence Compound where he used to work for Crake. Toby and Ren passively cling to the hope that "there must be someone else left, though; [they] can't be the only [ones] on the planet," (Atwood[c] 5) as they remain imprisoned in the ruins. After some time, the bioartist Amanda rescues Ren from the club, and then Ren stumbles to Toby's spa. Draining the edible cosmetic products in AnooYoo, they engage in a search for food. These survivors' walking, sauntering, *wandering* across borders and various physical environments reify an alternative mode of democratic practice that enables resistance to hegemonic political institutions (Fiskio 137). This is not to say that they raise the banner of revolution. On the contrary, their narratives end rather ambiguously. Apprehended and put on trial in the Five Kingdoms, Amedea suddenly burst into fire and from her charred remains flutters a locust (Bobis 173-4). An estranged Jimmy, Toby, and Ren, with Amanda and the two rebels, camp near the Carkers' settlement, and the last thing they hear is "the sound of many people singing" (431). These survivors may not have been able to enact palpable change in these Anthropocenes, but, through a form of return, the four are able to embody a novel and much-needed principle of living—specifically of eating, if I may add.

At the end of *Locust Girl*, Amedea attempts to fathom her role in the disarrayed world. Her retreat, which spans the Five Kingdoms and the wasteland, enable her to return to a firmer sense of identity: "*I am Amdea, daughter of Alkesta and Abarama / I am Beena, beloved of Beenabe / I am Locust Girl, kin to Cho-choli, Daninen, Espra / Fau-us, Gurimar, Haraharan, Inige, Just-me-uhm / Karitase, Lumi, Maritreses, Nartireses, Opi, Padumana / Quxik, Rirean, Silam, Trapsta, Unre, Verompe / Wildimus, Xuqik, Ycasa, Zacarem* [...] Oh how sweet it is — how sweet to remember all who have touched us" she sings (174, emphasis in original). Amedea develops a selfhood constituted by the humans who have contributed to her — for the lack of a better term — evolution. All throughout the narrative, Amedea unknowingly plays the role of the host — not only of the locust but also of the voices that are unheard (173). At this point, she recognises herself as a conduit of historical consciousness in the class antagonism of Bobis' Anthropocene.

The intertwined narratives of *Oryx and Crake* and *The Year of the Flood*, on the other hand, culminate in a poignant feast night (Atwood[c] 430). Through this nicety, we get a glimpse on how both Toby and Ren have changed throughout their retreat to solitude. Despite the pandemic that continues to threaten human life, the unlikely company finds solace and oneness with the forest environment. This harmony with nature seeps into mercy, demonstrated by Toby's insistence on sharing soup with Amanda's torturers.

By cultivating this framework, the three novels dramatise the possibility of restoration in the Anthropocene. They depict an Anthropocene that is finally aware of itself, and this means that "we can no longer think of ecological and economic cycles independently: the water; carbon; nitrogen; weather; and economic cycles of production, exchange, and waste are [all] interconnected" (Sullivan 49). As explicated in the preceding section, the novels suggest that eating is a monstrous activity as it fetishises a spate of ecological and political-economic crises driven by aggressive neoliberalist food production. By navigating through the narratives through the post-pastoral trope, we realise that they teach us how to eat restoratively as well. A sense of self and place in an ecological community—espoused by the novels' treatment of our species with the same exploitative attitude we have towards food—asks us to reconceptualise eating: there must be a problem in how food is culturally perceived, economically distributed, and ethically consumed in the Anthropocene.

Ultimately, *Locust Girl*, *Oryx and Crake*, and *The Year of the Flood*, by sharpening our perception of food ecopolitics, can become powerful forums where the ecological community can be imagined. These pastoral-perceptions impart such a framework through a scale-crossing environmental consciousness, tying issues of food, politics, and ecology from the bodily scale, to the local (species), and to the global (the planet). In forming counternarratives against neoliberal geopolitics which forcibly binds local food systems with the global, we can refer to texts such as these that prescribe a more pleasurable connection with our troubled world. This is not to say that literature can be a panacea to our environmental crises, or that they can be used as cases against agro-industrial TNC's like Monsanto. Nevertheless, as ecotopian fiction, Atwood and Bobis' committed visions of the Anthropocene are warnings, and warnings imply that readers have a choice. Literature's scale-crossing vision of the future stirs us to cultivate this consciousness before our minds annihilate all that is made to but a green thought, or as in Bobis' world, the rumor of green trees, and "green was [once] tall and proud" (4). We can start by reimagining the geopolitical context of our dinners. As Atwood's Gardeners recite, listen to "Nature's green applause— / Such will restore us" (Atwood[c] 405).

Works cited

Atwood[a], Margaret. *Oryx and Crake*. Anchor, 2004.

⸻[b]. *The Robber Bride*. Virago, 1994.

⸻[c]. *The Year of the Flood*. Anchor, 2009.

Barthes, Roland. "Toward a Psychosociology of Contemporary Food Consumption." *Food and Culture: A Reader*, ed. Carole Counihan & Penny Van Esterik, Routledge, 2008, pp. 28–35.

Bobis, Merlinda. *Locust Girl: A Lovesong*. Anvil Publishing, 2015.

Carruth, Allison. *Global Appetites: American Power and the Literature of Food*. Cambridge University Press, 2013.

Cotgrove, Steven. "Environmentalism and utopia." *The Sociological Review*, vol. 24, no. 1, pp. 23-42.

Crutzen, Paul & Eugene Stoermer. "The 'Anthropocene'." *Global Change Newsletter*, no. 41, 200, pp. 17-8.

Evernden, Neil. "Beyond Ecology: Self, Place, and the Pathetic Fallacy." *The Ecocriticism Reader: Landmarks in Literary Ecology*, ed. Cheryll Glotfelty and Harold Fromm, University of Georgia Press, 1996, pp. 92-103.

Fiskio, Janet. "Sauntering Across the Border: Thoreau, Nabhan, and Food Politics." *The Cambridge Companion to Literature and the Environment*, ed. Louise Westling, Cambridge University Press, 2013, pp. 136-151.

Gifford, Terry. "Pastoral, Anti-Pastoral, and Post-Pastoral." *The Cambridge Companion to Literature and the Environment*, ed. Louise Westling, Cambridge University Press, 2013, pp. 17-30.

Hengen, Shannon. "Margaret Atwood and environmentalism." *The Cambridge Companion to Margaret Atwood*, ed. Carol Ann Howells, Cambridge University Press, 2006, pp. 72-85.

Howells, Coral Ann. "Margaret Atwood's dystopian visions: *The Handmaid's Tale* and *Oryx and Crake*." *The Cambridge Companion to Margaret Atwood*, ed. Carol Ann Howells, Cambridge University Press, 2006, pp. 161-175.

Kershaw, Baz. "Projecting climate scenarios, landscaping nature, and knowing performance: on becoming performed by ecology." *Green Letters: Studies in Ecocriticism*, vol. 20, no. 3, 2016, pp. 270-289.

Loomba, Ania. *Colonialism/Postcolonialism* (3rd edition). Routledge, 2015.

McKibben[a], Bill. *Enough: Genetic Engineering and the End of Human Nature*. Bloomsbury, 2004.

⸻[b]. "What the Warming World Needs Now is Art, Sweet Art." *Grist*, 22 April 2005. Accessed 29 Sept. 2017.

Moylan, Thomas. *Scraps of the Untainted Sky: Science Fiction, Utopia, Dystopia*. Westview Press, 2000.

Omeje, Kenneth. "Extractive Economies and Conflicts in the Global South: Re-Engaging Rentier Theory and Politics." *Extractive Economies and Conflicts in the Global South Multi-Regional Perspectives on Rentier Politics*, ed. Kenneth Omeje, Ashgate, pp. 1-26.

Pressley, Cindy. "Using Ecotopian Fiction to Reimagine Public Policy: From a Resource-Based Narrative to a Competing Values Narrative." *Administrative Theory & Praxis*, vol., vol.7, no. 2, 2015, pp. 111-126.

Ridout, Alice. "Margaret Atwood's Straddling Environmentalism." *Comparative American Studies: An International Journal*, vol. 13, no. 2, 2015, pp. 31-41.

Romero, Paolo. "Expert warns of possible food shortage in Philippines." *Philstar Global*, 29 Nov. 2017, http://www.philstar.com/agriculture/2015/11/29/1526943/expert-warns-possible-food-shortage-Philippines. Accessed 8 Oct. 2017.

Sommerville, Melanie, Jamey Essex & Philippe Le Billon. "The 'Global Food Crisis' and the Geopolitics of Food Security." *Geopolitics*, vol. 19, no. 2, 2014, pp. 239-265.

Sullivan, Heather. "The dark pastoral: Goethe and Atwood." *Green Letters: Studies in Ecocriticism*, vol. 20, no. 1, 2016, pp. 47-59.

Sussex, Lucy. "*Locust Girl: A Lovesong*—In fantasy, Merlinda Bobis exposes real-world truths." *The Sunday Morning Herald*, 9 Aug. 2015. Accessed 23 Sept. 2017.

Sze, Julie. "Environmental Justice Anthropocene Narratives: Sweet Art, Recognition,

Representation." *Resilience: A Journal of the Environmental Humanities*, vol. 2, no. 2, 2014, pp. 103-118.

The Economist Intelligence Unit. "Global Food Security Suffers its First Deterioration in Five Years." 2017. Accessed 12 October 2017.

Vials, Chris. "Margaret Atwood's dystopic fiction and the contradictions of neoliberal freedom." *Textual Practice*, vol. 29, no. 2, 2015, pp. 235-254.

Weis, Tony. *The global food economy: the battle for the future of farming*. Zed Books, 2007.

Wilson, Edward. *The Future of Life*. Knopf, 2002.

Chapter 4

A Return to Innocence: Encountering the Numinous in Children's Fantasy Fiction by Cyan Abad-Jugo

Gabriela Lee,
University of the Philippines, Philippines

Abstract

From 2011 to 2014, Cyan Abad-Jugo, a Filipino writer for children and young adults, came out with a series of stories that were published, in chapters, in the *Philippine Daily Inquirer*'s Learning Section. These stories were eventually gathered into four chapter books and published as a set by Anvil Publishing, Inc. in 2016. All four stories feature child protagonists encountering a series of problems in their environment — whether urban or rural — and, through a series of fantastical and supernatural events, find a way to solve the mystery. Throughout the stories, there is a particular sense of wonder in the world, or what Brawley, Palumbo, and Sullivan term as the "numinous," which they then apply to mythopoeic fantasy stories — of which children's literature has in abundance.

In using the concept of the numinous to read Cyan Abad-Jugo's set of four chapter books for children, I argue that the fantastical elements of the narratives allow the child protagonists to transcend their physical and social limitations and directly impact their environments in a positive and empowering manner. In doing so, this paper presentation will return to the oldest forms of children's stories — myths and legends — and how they are retold and retooled for a contemporary generation, in the hopes that by building on that sense of wonder in the natural world, today's children may begin their own transformations.

Keywords: fantasy, children's literature, Philippine literature, ecology.

The personification of nature, and the symbolic actions taken by these personifications of nature, is a common trope in fantasy fiction. Brian Attebery, a noted fantasy scholar, says that "[t]he fundamental premise of fantasy is that the things it tells not only did not happen but could not have happened. In that literal untruth is freedom to tell many symbolic truths without forcing a choice among them" (15). It is this symbolic truth that is useful for the fantasy reader, because by elevating the fantastical idea towards the symbolic, the concept is imbued with meaning that can resonate beyond the constraints of the literal and the real. For instance, in *The Lord of the Rings*, JRR Tolkien's creation of the Ents provides them with the fictional opportunity to confront the very human destruction of their forests. In this manner, Tolkien engages in the kind of fantasy that "traces the unsaid and the unseen of culture: that which has been silenced, made invisible, covered over and made 'absent'" (Jackson 4, qtd. in Brawley 11). This engagement with, a kind of rootedness in, the natural world can be seen in other modern works of fantasy, such as *The Earthsea Quartet* by Ursula K. LeGuin, *The Chronicles of Thomas Covenant* by Stephen R. Donaldson, and *Redwall* by Brian Jacques, among many others.

Furthermore, through the act of reading fantasy, the reader is exposed to "authors who are employing fantasy as a subversive mode of literature to revise our perceptions of the natural world; and, the distinguishing feature of these authors is going to be an inculcation of a certain religious or mystical 'feeling' of the numinous in the reader" (Brawley 6). In particular, fantasy genre subverts the reader's expectations and experiences of reality, as "[t]his transformation of ordinary reality [into fantasy] is made possible through the infusion of the numinous. In short, the [fantasy] author undertakes two tasks: to instill awareness of the transcendent, and to turn that awareness back to the mundane world" (Brawley 17). It is this act of encountering the numinous in fantasy that becomes an impetus for the reader to act in preserving its source: the natural world.

The concept of the numinous in fantasy literature is derived from the writings of Rudolf Otto, who argues "that quality of 'holiness' in its original meaning as that which inspires awe... the numinous consciousness can be evoked through means of symbols which objectify the numinous state of mind. These symbols act as vehicles of the numinous consciousness, concretizing it within rational forms" (Otto 6-7, qtd. in Brawley 15). Fantasy is full of symbolic worlds, creatures, and actions that subvert reality and it is through this subversion that the numinous comes alive. In fact, it is through the act of creating fantasy worlds that "fantasy's capacity for mythopoiesis [is revealed]: the making of narratives that reshape the world" (Attebery 21). In particular, "[m]ythopoeic fantasy offers, especially with its functions of subverting normative categories of thought (Jackson) and revising the way reality is perceived (Hume), a valid means whereby environmental perception may be addressed" (Brawley 23). Mythopoesis, as used in fantasy fiction, provides the reader with a lens with which to examine the natural world from another, defamiliarised angle.

However, fantasy fiction is also commonly seen as fiction exclusively for children, or considered juvenile fiction, with all the attendant negativity the term implies. For instance, Booker Prize-winning author AS Byatt wrote a scathing indictment of the *Harry Potter* series and its adult readers in *The New York Times*, whom she considers "childish" and unable to move on from such immature pursuits. The rich tradition of children's fantasy seems to give this kind of thinking a particular credence: the tradition of fantasy is "clearly central to any understanding of children's literature. Some have argued that fantasy is the very core of children's literature, and that children's literature did not properly exist until the imagination had been given an entirely free rein to entertain children in unreservedly fantastical books … it has also been argued that all children's literature is necessarily a fantasy" (Grenby 144-145). As Tolkien himself also asserts, in his seminal essay "On Fairy-Stories," "[i]t is usually assumed that children are the natural or the specially appropriate audience for fairy-stories" (4). However, he also points out that this is not intentional, but rather an "accident of our domestic history" (4) where stories of the fantastic are relegated to the nursery from the Victorian era onwards by adults who did not seem to find a use for such stories. In more recent scholarship, Mendelsohn and Levy note that "the history of children's fantasy is essentially one of appropriation, both children appropriating texts, and those who have written for children... appropriating and adapting the material for children" (11) throughout literature, history, and the arts; this ultimately questions Byatt's narrow-minded argument against the literary and cultural value of children's fantasy fiction.

However, it is precisely the capability of fantasy fiction for mythopoesis that makes it uniquely suitable for children and adult readers. In providing an opportunity to experience the numinous in fantastic fiction, the child reader is elevated and empowered by imagining themselves to be part of the narrative — the hero or heroine, "becom[ing] powerful and important figures, although in their real worlds they have been weak" (Grenby 159-160). By yoking myth to fantasy, where "writers... incorporate structures and motifs from recorded texts of oral culture... [and] make[s] sure that the reader will respond to the fantastic" (Attebery, 8), the reader's experience with the narrative becomes numinous — bridging the old with the new, the ancient with the contemporary. It is this kind of literary empowerment that is necessary if we are to try and teach young readers of the need to preserve the natural world for their own and future generations. By giving the individual reader the experience of the numinous in reading fantasy fiction, they are allowed to imagine what can be done if they succeed in saving the environment, and the consequences of what might happen if they do not contribute to such efforts.

In Myra Garces-Bacsal's survey of award-winning children's books in the Philippines, she noted that fantasy comprised 19% of the books that have won a national award, compared to 54% of the books, which used contemporary realist mode (95). It can also be observed that the tradition of using the fantastic mode of writing in children's literature has become unpopular in recent decades. Whenever it is used, it becomes a vehicle to educate and empower children to be conscious of, and aid in the preservation of, the natural world. Examples of these books, published between the 1980s and the 1990s, would be *Si Pilandok, ang Bantay ng Kalikasan* ("Pilandok, the Guardian of Nature") by Virgilio S. Almario and Kora Dandan-Albano, *Ang Hukuman ni Sinukan* ("The Justice of Sinukan") by Virgilio S. Almario and Mitzi Villacer, and *Si Emang Engakntada at ang Tatlong Haragan* ("Emma the Fairy and the Three Naughty Children") by Rene O. Villanueva, Alfonso Oñate, and Wilfredo Pollarco. One of the more contemporary continuations of these fantasy traditions for younger readers is a series of chapbooks from author Cyan Abad-Jugo. From 2011 to 2014, she came out with a series of stories that were published, in chapters, in the *Philippine Daily Inquirer*'s Learning Section. These stories were eventually gathered into four chapter books and published as a set by Anvil Publishing, Inc. in 2016. They are *Yaya Maya and the White King, The Earth-Healers, Letters from Crispin,* and *The Looking-Glass Tree.*

All four stories feature child protagonists encountering a series of problems in their environment — whether urban or rural — and, through a series of fantastical and supernatural events, find a way to solve the problem. The inciting incident of each story focuses on the protagonists' first encounter with the numinous: a talking frog, the ability to shrink to the size of a mouse, or taking to the air with a heron. Each moment of magical transformation is accompanied by a choice: help the natural world regain balance or stand aside and watch its destruction. In using the concept of the numinous to read Cyan Abad-Jugo's set of four chapter books for children, we can see how the fantastical elements of the narratives allow the child protagonists to transcend their physical and social limitations and empower them to directly impact their natural environments in a positive manner.

Similar to Tolkien's creation of the Ents, three of the four chapbooks by Abad-Jugo feature personified natural elements such as trees, mountains, the earth, and animals. In *Yaya Maya and the White King*, the protagonist Ina battles the forces of the White King and the White Queen, who are personifications of white termites, by taking on the persona of the mountain diwata, Mayang or Mariang Makiling. What is unusual about this story is that it is not about man's encroachment on nature, but rather two distinct forces of nature trying to encroach on one another. Here, the narrative provides a reversal of the trope of the benevolent forces of nature, when, during the climax of the story, Ina (as Mayang) encounters the White Queen, who orchestrated the invasion of their land:

> "Do we have to fight? Why can't you just learn to live with us? There is so much space here," Ina said, remembering how empty she thought the neighborhood had been.
> "Because it is the land that I want, not neighbors," [said the White Queen].
> "It ... it isn't your land."
> The queen stood up ... "It's mine now. Even your power is mine." (Abad-Jugo 59-60).

In providing both benevolent and destructive personifications of nature, *Yaya Maya* shows that nature requires a delicate balance between benign and rampant growth and that nature is cyclical rather than linear. By placing the child protagonist in between a battle of who can lay claim over the land, this story allows for a deeper understanding of homeostasis and equilibrium in the natural world. Furthermore,

Similarly, the conflict over land ownership is present in *The Earth-Healers*, where the concept of tectonic plates is personified by sleeping giants. These giants are lulled to sleep by small creatures known as Earth-Healers, whose lullabies keep the giants slumbering. However, whenever the giants are awakened by man-made disturbances, they become the cause of earthquakes and volcanic eruptions. Jopi, the protagonist, was chosen by the tree spirits to be the voice of the natural world, to change the mind of the Mayor of the town, whose drill kept on destroying the mountains and waking the giants in his efforts to find more gold.

> "An earthquake... which could destroy Mount Zoilo, and set off volcanoes, or unleash the river in your town. We can't predict what will happen, but the results will be the same."
> "Many deaths. Much suffering." Thetys kneeled and faced Jopi. There was a bald patch around her eyes, which made her look sad and

tired. "The Mayor's drill, he has drive it in too deep. We can't hold out much longer, we are growing weak, and the giants are wounding and waking" (Abad-Jugo 40).

Much like in Ina in *Yaya Maya*, Jopi encounters the numinous through an animal mediator — in this case, their neighbor's pet cow. He is gifted with borrowed powers from the Earth-Healers — the spirits of the animals, trees, and the land — and who was tasked to save his town from destruction, since "[t]his had already happened to other villages in the country. It was why the tree-spirits were so sad, mourning for the folk they had lost in these villages" (Abad-Jugo, 61). It is clear that nature does not seek to harm humanity, and in the story, even the nature spirits mourn the loss of human lives in the destruction of lands. Here, the cycle of destruction was begun by humans; it could only be ended by humans as well. Jopi's success at stopping the Mayor's destructive mining methods meant that the town's natural resources could flourish once more.

The question of choice also occurs in *The Looking-Glass Tree*. Much like in the first two books, the protagonist, Enrico, encounters the numinous through his experience in a mangrove forest. When his aunt illegally uproots a mangrove sapling from a protected grove in order to sell it to her clients, Enrico — with the help of the spirit of the mangrove tree, Aninipot, and her wetland creatures — has to bring the sapling and the spirit back to her grove before Aninipot unleashes a storm across the islands.

> Ani turned to him. Her eyes shone, and a ring of fireflies sparkled around her head. "Scattered like leaves in the forest, driven apart by my storm."
> "Your storm? Are you causing it?" Enrico asked.
> Ani shrugged. "They have to learn their lesson."
> Enrico crawled close to her feet. "Couldn't we just talk to them first? Make them understand?" (Abad-Jugo 61)

Just like in the previous books, the child character attempts to bargain with the nature spirits, before finally using their own wits and imagination to change the course of destruction wrought by both humans and nature. In this case, Enrico bargains with the spirits of nature to show mercy to the mangrove poachers — including his own aunt — and to shift from punishment to educating people why it is necessary to allow nature to flourish on its own.

The final book, *Letters From Crispin*, deviates from the first three books, in that it does not use the obvious presence of the natural world within the story, and yet the numinous is still present in the way that the narrative progresses. In this story, which takes place in August 1986, during the aftermath of the People Power Revolution in the Philippines, young Alice arrives at her great-grandmother's home in Caloocan City for her 100th birthday. During her explorations, she comes across a hollow in an old tree, where she begins receiving letters from a young boy named Crispin, who lived in 1896, at the height of the Philippine Revolution against the Spanish colonial forces. Through exchanging letters with the boy, Alice learns about the nature of her own national identity, and what the people around her are fighting for — the opportunity for freedom.

Unlike in the other books, Alice is not asked to fight against an obvious threat against the natural world, but simply the threat of time, loss of memory, and forgetting. This act of remembering and reclamation is an important aspect of fantasy fiction, since the character becomes what Carl von Sydow calls "the memorate, which is an eyewitness account of an encounter with extraordinary or numinous forces... Memorates are realistic narratives about magical narratives; so too are many works of modern fantasy" (Attebery 16). Towards the end of the story, we learn that Crispin was really writing to his young beloved, Alicia — the great-grandmother for whom Alice was named for. It is through this act of remembrance that both great-grandmother and great-granddaughter fight against the ravages of time and remember, and celebrate:

> "People waved red banners instead of yellow ribbons. Perhaps it doesn't matter what the colors are. We must remember, instead, that the Filipinos are worth fighting for. That's what my own son and daughter-in-law believed in, and died for, in the seventies. That's what my granddaughters and grandson-in-law believe now, and teach to my great-granddaughter. We must always celebrate the Filipino spirit" (Abad-Jugo 63).

In fact, all four protagonists occupy the position of the memorate in their respective narratives, which allows them not only to experience the numinous, but to become repositories of these narratives. The stories end with the expectation that they will be able to continue occupying the world between the fantastic and the real, and become protectors of both. In these stories, the numinous becomes the solidifying experience for the children to realise the value of the natural world, and why it needs protecting.

All four books therefore provide a way for the child reader to anchor themselves to the idea that although they are children, they have the capacity to carry on, or to continue, the path that has been laid out by the natural world. The numinous presences in all four narratives — Mariang Makiling, the spirit of the mountain, in *Yaya Maya*; the Earth-Healers and the giants in

The Earth-Healers; Aninipot, the spirit of the mangrove trees in *The Looking-Glass Tree*; and the spirit of Crispin on the eve of the 1898 Philippine Revolution in *Letters From Crispin* — provide a way for the protagonists to access the natural world on their own terms. The protagonists' experiences allow for growth, through their own understanding of the world around them and their place within it. This positionality allows them to take ownership of the environment they live in: the oceans and the mountains, the towns and cities that shape their lives. By providing these children with a way to understand, access, and take ownership of their environment, they are then given an opportunity to respond.

As we can see, throughout the four books, this aspect of the numinous becomes necessary in order to instigate that call to action that is necessary for the child protagonists to act. Each protagonist is emboldened to act despite their own misgivings and uncertainties — both with the fantastical occurrences and with themselves. This is the case "[i]n children's fantasy writing, [where Todorov's] uncertainty is often personified in the text by a leading character, who represents the readers and their responses to the strangeness" (Grenby 151). The character Enrico clearly articulates this thought that many young people have perhaps thought about during moments of helplessness against the face of a greater and more powerful force: "What could a boy like him do?" (Abad-Jugo 45). The four books all respond, in various ways, to this question.

As seen through Abad-Jugo's four works, it is through fantasy fiction that we can see how the child reader can locate and empower themselves within the broader socio-cultural conversations about environmentalism and the preservation of the natural world that surround them. Even though "fantasy writing is, by definition, generally disengaged from reality, it is often easy to discern its entanglement in the ideological controversies of its day. This may be, of course, because fantasy so readily invites symbolic readings" (Grenby 154), which allows the child reader to have nuance in terms of approaching the problem of environmental degradation and any potential roles they might have in preventing these problems from accelerating.

In these four stories, the child reader can easily step into the shoes of the child characters and anchor themselves in the stories that provide them a chance to *do* something as opposed to simply passively observe and allow things to happen to them. This kind of fantasy is what Grenby terms as "'Ptolemaic' fantasy, the world revolving around the protagonist as Ptolemy thought the sun, stars and planets revolved around the Earth" (159-160), which is useful in both establishing a child's individuality and active role in society. In particular, this kind of "[f]antasy is extremely well suited to consideration of questions of identity... the form eminently suitable for the transmission of lessons on selfhood, these being regarded now as the best kind of instruction that good children's literature can and should teach" (Grenby 164). This is why fantasy is "both empowering or disorientating for protagonists and readers" (Grenby 166). However, Ptolemaic fantasy is useful in this regard because the attention is centered on the child protagonist and their individualised encounter with the numinous.

In providing the child reader with an opportunity to encounter the numinous, Abad-Jugo's children's fantasy fiction allows what Cheryl Glotfelty says is "the fundamental premise that human culture is connected to the physical world, affecting it and affected by it. [These] interconnections between nature and culture, specifically the cultural artifacts language and literature… negotiates between the human and the nonhuman." In remembering the experience of the numinous, these protagonists become carriers of memory. And through these negotiations between magic and memory that the numinous occurs and is experienced in fantasy, which in turn, can empower the child reader to act on behalf of the natural world.

Works Cited

Abad-Jugo, Cyan. *Yaya Maya and the White King*. Anvil Publishing, Inc., 2016.

--- . *The Earth-Healers*. Anvil Publishing, Inc., 2016.

--- . *Letters from Crispin*. Anvil Publishing, Inc., 2016.

--- . *The Looking-Glass Tree*. Anvil Publishing, Inc., 2016.

Adarna House. *Adarna House Book Guide 2018*. https://drive.google.com/file/d/0B2MUzoUzt0L-NzhNQzNhdDIyTlU/view. Accessed May 31, 2018.

Attebery, Brian. *Stories About Stories: Fantasy and the Remaking of Myth*. Oxford University Press, 2014.

--- . *Strategies of Fantasy*. Indiana University Press, 1994.

Brawley, Chris, et al. *Nature and the Numinous in Mythopoeic Fantasy Literature*. McFarland & Company, 2016.

Byatt, A.S. "Harry Potter and the Childish Adult." *The New York Times*, July 7, 2003. https://www.nytimes.com/2003/07/07/opinion/harry-potter-and-the-childish-adult.html. Accessed May 31, 2018.

Glotfelty, Cheryl. "What is Ecocriticism?" *Defining Ecocritical Theory and Practice: 16 Position Papers from the 1994 Western Literature Association Meeting*. Salt Lake City, 1994.

Grenby, Matthew. *Children's Literature*. Edinburgh University Press, 2008.

Levy, Michael, and Farah Mendlesohn. *Children's Fantasy Literature: An Introduction*. Cambridge University Press, 2014.

Chapter 5

"Escaping from the Anxiety, Returning to the Field"[1]: Nostalgia in Nguyen Quang Thieu's Ecological Poems

Dang Thi Bich Hong,
Hung Vuong University, Vietnam

Abstract

In the early 1990s, literary researchers promoted the linkages between literature with environmental issues, creating a new approach: ecological critique. This critique was born as a reaction to environmental threats in the context of modern society, when mankind faced countless global ecological disasters. The eco-discourse in literature is widely used in many countries around the world. East Asia is a region with a tradition of respect for nature. However, this area is also facing more serious environmental problems in the modern era. Vietnam does not stand out from the regional ecological emergency. Therefore, the ecological literature has appeared and is more clearly shaped. The subject of ecology enters the works by most famous contemporary Vietnamese writers. Nguyen Quang Thieu belongs to the generation of the writers who are famous after the renovation in 1986. Sensitive to change in life, Nguyen Quang Thieu's poetry has many concerns about ecology. The poems yearning for "escaping from the anxiety, returning to the field" are the desire to come back home and return to childhood and to the beautiful values of human and non-human worlds.

---

[1] This is a poem line in "The Field" by Nguyen Quang Thieu. In this paper, Nguyen Quang Thieu's verses were cited from the collection entitled *The Delta* that was published by Writers' Association Publishing House in 2010.

Keywords: Nguyen Quang Thieu, *The Delta*, ecology, nostalgia, urban place, hometown.

Rationale

Ecology as a biology-related science at first studies the interaction between creatures and their habitat. The proponent of the term "ecology" is Ernst Haeckel.[2] In the second half of the twentieth century, mankind faced countless global ecological disasters. The United Nations Summit, held in Rio de Janeiro (Brazil) in June 1992, set the goal of sustainable development in order to call for worldwide attention on the ecological environment and climate change including global warming, desertification, and sea level rise. Consequently, ecology which affects many different sciences forms ecological philosophy, ecological politics, ecological economics, and ecological psychology. Christopher Manes writes in "Nature and Silence" (University of Georgia Press, 1996) that:

> Nature is silent in our culture ... in the sense that the status of a speaking subject is jealously guarded as an exclusively human prerogative... The language we speak... veils the processes of nature with its own cultural obsessions, directionalities, and motifs that have no analogies in the natural world. (15)

In the field of humanities, researchers of literary studies have also promoted the link between literary activities and environmental issues, creating a new approach that is ecological critique.

The eco-discourse in literature is widely used in many countries around the world. East Asia is a region with a tradition of respect for nature. This governs how people form their attitudes or principles of dealing with the natural world. Literature of East Asia, therefore, is famous for its compositions which praise the beauty of nature and depict attachments and harmonious relationships between man and nature. However, this area is also facing more serious environmental problems in the modern era. Simon Estok in *Partial Views: An Introduction to East Asian Ecocriticisms* (Palgrave Macmillan, 2013) argues that:

---

[2] The term "ecology" was coined by the German biologist *Ernst Haeckel* in *Generelle Morphologie der Organismen* (Berlin: G. Reimer, 1866). He defined it as the relation of the animal both to its organic as well as its inorganic environment.

East Asian ecocriticisms address urgent problems (some unique to the region, others less so) regardless of whether the West listens or wants to listen. The rapid postwar industrialization currently progressing in the region poses perhaps the most immediate social and environmental challenges. (2)

Vietnam does not stand out from the regional ecological emergency. Wars which lasted for 30 years have left heavy and long-lasting consequences on the environment. Industrialisation and modernisation have resulted in many challenges to the environment such as air pollution, soil pollution, and ocean pollution. In that situation, the ecological literature has appeared and is more clearly shaped. The subject of ecology enters the works by most famous contemporary Vietnamese writers.

Nguyen Quang Thieu (1957) belongs to the generation of the writers who are famous after the renovation. In this period, literature transits from the epic trend to the one of life inspiration in which everyday life with the simplest emotions is reflected. Sensitive to changes in life, Nguyen Quang Thieu's poetry has many concerns about ecology. The poet realises that the people in the modern world are gradually losing nature, losing their memories about the village and losing themselves. From an ecological perspective, Nguyen Quang Thieu's poetry yearning for "escaping from the anxiety, returning to the field" is the desire to come back home and return to childhood and to the beautiful values of human and non-human worlds. Hidden in the new words and images, Nguyen Quang Thieu's poetry is the journey back to the traditional spiritual values of the nation and humankind as a whole.

Urban Place: Expatriation and the Separation from Nature

The emergence of urban life is a special event in the history of human culture. On the one hand, the city is the administrative unit that marks the development of society. On the other hand, the building of cities depicts God's ambition of building the world. In the Bible, the city is a place of vices and excess pride. The punishment and the confusion of languages during the construction of the tower of Babel divided people into opposing groups. They do not speak the same languages; therefore, they do not understand one other and then do not sympathise.

From an ecological perspective, urban life leads to a bad consequence which separates people from the natural world. Thus, ecological composition and critique in many countries are associated with the development of industrial civilisation and modern cities. Famous romantic writers such as George Byron and Alphonse Daudet have brought into focus on breaking with cities. Thus, poetry comes back to the countryside and new regions (Hubbell; Bang). *Walden* was written by Henry David Thoreau when the United States was in the development of capitalism. People chose to turn their back on the "American dream" with luxuries and material comforts, coming into the forest alone to experience life in harmony with nature (Thoreau). In China, ecological literature emerged when people witness the chimneys which discharged smokes into the environment seriously polluted the urban atmosphere. Vietnamese literature in the early twentieth century began to mention the uncertainty of urban life. Until the 1990s when the country moved quickly into the urbanisation, people often experienced feelings of being both excited about living in the city and afraid of it.

In East Asian writers' view, urban space is also a course of driftage. With the people born in, growing up from the village and attached to the millennial agricultural civilisation, the countryside becomes a symbol of peace, happiness and protection. Separation from the countryside means the experience of extreme loneliness. Nguyen Quang Thieu's poetry is obsessed with a sense of exile. "Road" is a symbol of boundary space with the hometown on one side and the bitterness on the other:

> Far
> Away from the road
> A person walks, a person walks, a person walks
> Just steps and stumbles
> [...]
> Hometown
> Hidden behind the clouds
> Hometown in the wind
> I can not wipe all afternoon rain
> To see clearly.
> ("Expatriation", *The Delta*, 85)

"The road" divides the journey of the exile into two opposing halves: in the front is the remote distance, the destruction, and the loss; behind is the scent of vanishing old homeland. Behind the words there is a stunned face looking at the old homeland, seeking a spiritual refuge. But "cloud", "wind", "afternoon rain" of the strange land increase human being's helplessness in dealing with inevitable separation: although the homeland is still there, it suddenly becomes distant and unreachable. Therefore, "Expatriation" also means losing a shelter and falling into bitterness!

Nguyen Quang Thieu's poems, since *The Insomnia of Fire*, have many times mentioned "to leave home," "far from hometown," "lost." On the journey of "missing steps," majestic nature does not relieve a person's mind but fills him with sorrow:

> There's only one more round
> The sun will touch the sea
> That's when my heart hurts
> That's when I can not stand it
> When a missing song comes back
>   ("Sunset Sonata in the Sea", *The Delta*, 40)

Sunset is the moment when exilic feelings are easily awoken in the soul of the exile who is lonely and has a desire to come back. His poems are like words of confession about the expatriation. The attraction of poetry, after all, lies in the sincerity of the emotions, first of all, it is the poet's sincerity when facing his own emotions. When composing poems as an action of confessing, man no longer sees the self as a symbol of power. The self then becomes a fragile being with both happiness and pain as well.

Writing about the space of cultures out of Chua village, Nguyen Quang Thieu includes a lot of the ups-and-downs of urban life. The country has been changing in the direction of poverty. Many values are in a big change. The most noticeable thing here is the absence of nature. The cities in Nguyen Quang Thieu's poetry are associated with desire, values matter and unpredictability. In "The Ants through the Banquet" (*The Delta*, 77), the world is described as "a messy party", "a gust of whirlwind from the ceiling fan" and "a 1000 watt light bulb — the pretended sun". These make the little creatures in the natural world "have teary eyes / hold hands taking each other to the deep caves". Specifically, poor ants try to find food from dishes, cups, and pieces of meat ... But "banquet" is not a space for them; what they receive is not fulfillment but bitterness. Then, the little ants lonely and tiredly return to their "deep caves", where they truly belong to. The life of ants is also the destiny of human beings in their harsh existence. The sounds of cities are described to be chaotic and deceitful.

> The town, light went out at night
> Someone cried out
> Someone laughed with chokes
> Someone covered his side of vulgarity with the darkness
> The other side with flickering fireflies.
>   ("The Sail", *The Delta*, 73)

In "End-of-the-day Questions" (*The Delta*, 80), a corner of the city without nature and full of dull rhythms, is portrayed in an insensible way: I "wait for the train to stop", the leaves "fall" and the afternoon rain "rises". Through the dream and reality of the lyrical character, urban life emerges with two opposing sides, one with "beautiful girls in skirts ride motorbikes" and the other with "the girl peddlers sit sleeping/ Hair and clothes full of dried fish smell". The country is changing but life is pushed to the extremes, and it still remains the heart-rending taste. Beautiful girls with "skirts" and "motorbikes" are associated with advances in material lives. But, such economic advantage misses some groups of people; they are trafficking girl in trucks which are "creaky and dirty like giant duck cages". Economic hardships turn their dreams. Into deadly deserts) "End-of-the-day Questions" are the questions about the marriage: "If I marry them/ How do I sleep with them?". As the world and its culture are changing, the questions are a symbol of a great marriage of life values. Human beings are thrown into this marriage with a lonely mood to enter it.

The urbanisation with the influence of the material life results in the forgotten nature. Nature is both the victim and the witness of the win-lose in this process. It is no longer the backdrop of human life but becomes an independent entity with its own losses and pains. All creatures "run and look up at the trees struggling to spout"; especially, the birds beat their wings unsteadily and singing a song of patience" the clouds become heavier because "the dust which tries to struggle with the weather allergy; and:

> At the new — peeled stars — infants' eyes, wine drops of the hope
> At the wind river flowing between the sides of the hoarsed throat of the night
> At the souls of the killed lakes that are hovering to look for the landing place.
> ("The Prayer", *The Delta*, 120)

Natural creatures occur in vulnerable and miserable forms: "the trees struggling to spout", the flock of birds walk unsteadily and blowzily' "birds beating their wings unsteadily", clouds are filled with dust "Clouds due to the dust", and "river the sides of the hoarsed throat, and souls of lakes are killed... All are symbols of a natural world that is gradually losing its place in urban life.

Karen Thornber's *Ecoambiguity: Environmental Crises and East Asia Literatures* (University of Michigan Press, 2012) emphasised "the complex, contradictory interactions between people and environments with a significant nonhuman presence" (1). In Nguyen Quang Thieu's poems, as a paradox, urban life with so many material facilities created by man for his own life becomes the habitation of nonhuman values. Man cannot find his shelter in the seemly close and familiar space. (Plans, signatures, phones, rubber benches, birthday parties, knocks, the keys, the dishes, the cookbooks, the diapers, old clothes ... represent a convenient city life. Nevertheless, in Nguyen Quang Thieu's poem, they do not bring to human any sense of security. Urban life has become a frightening reality, where people cannot find any comfort. They are forced to flee, but the city has "no safe place for them to hide one finger" because it only has "gaunt dark alleys, tough curbs, diseased parks". Then, attempt to "escape from plans, signatures.... from the phones, from the rubber benches... from the birthday parties". They also strive to turn their minds away:

> from the knocks, the key
> from the dishes and the cookbooks
> from the diapers, old clothes exposed on the roofs of the city
> ("The Prayer", *The Delta*, 120)

With the sensitivity to listen to the voice of nature, Nguyen Quang Thieu anticipates the tragic consequences that humans will face. That is the flood, at which "the water is stronger than the explosion" resulting "on the table was full of fish bones. The water carriage is rolling toward us." And, people "see a bright bloody dawn hiding in the dark skin. Tonight, the water has come. With the great silence, the water immerges wingless things" ("A Witness of Death", Section 1, *The Delta*, 228)

Is it the day of the rise of the water world or the day when mankind faces extermination? The man isn't the hero of conquering nature. In that great flood, man is a victim, a witness and a perpetrator:

> From the flooded town
> They go upwards the bridge
> A man and a woman
> Have no clothes on their bodies
> As if they are just born
> ("A Witness of Death", Section 19, *The Delta*, 270)

Water provides human with living sources, but it can also destroy their lives. Images of a man and a woman in newborn figures, who witness "a flooded town", which signify the death of the town, and the dissolution of human life when nature is angry. "The rage of the blue sky" or the punishment by nature to man when he breaks the ecological balance. This fact is repeatedly said in Nguyen Quang Thieu's poetry and prose works. The man who leaves the city in Nguyen Quang Thieu's works realised that:

The heat from the sky pours down like a huge fire. The heat from various vehicles of the city blows out like a storm. The heat from the air-conditioned rooms and from the heads ... The heat is like a wild beast crazily hunting human beings.
(Nguyen Quang Thieu, *The Man Leaves the City*, 116).

Above all, people need "a place" to return.

When the earth is warming up
And the human heart is becoming cold
I need you, I need friends, I need trees
I need the hometown to return to myself
("Night Morning", *The Delta*, 100)

Nature and people change in opposite directions: the earth becomes "warm" while people's hearts become "colder". Nevertheless, these changes make people lose their peaceful nests in natural and spiritual worlds. In that situation, returning to homeland, and coming back to fresh green trees form the human's journeys of returning to their selves. The deep beauties of the homeland in connection with the pure natural world and the pure rural countryside in Vietnam form a characteristic in Nguyen Quang Thieu's ecological poems.

Nature and Feminity: the Deposit of Old Hometown

Each individual, despite his life's ups and downs, is connected to another one in a physical environment and has a certain "place-attachment". Each person has a vague relationship, both mysterious, sacred and powerful concerning his hometown. Old home in Nguyen Quang Thieu's poetry is not only a geographic space (with names of communes and villages in Vietnam) but also a cultural tradition. Nguyen Quang Thieu in his writing about Nguyen Binh, who is nationally considered the poet of Vietnamese countryside, shares that returning to the old hometown or more precisely speaking, returning to the origin of the nation, emerges after the first few decades of the urbanisation storm, when people realise that a lot of values of modern life are only temporary, confusing and uncertain. Returning home — the origin of the nation — is to return to what is simple, loving, pure, warm and safe, and to the pure beauty creating the Vietnamese cultural values. (Nguyen Quang Thieu, "Nguyen Binh's Poetry", 21-2). As a result, in Nguyen Quang Thieu's poems, hometown is not a purely peaceful rural area. It is also a place keeping memories which enriches the spiritual life.

In Nguyen Quang Thieu's poetry, the expatriate "steps but stumbles" brings with him their memories as luggage. The scene of Chua village and Day river with its wharfs, plains and fields comes and goes again and again. The odor of the motherland goes into the sleep: "Only the smell of dry faeces catching fire in the roadside / Puts the expatriate in to a bitter sleep" ("Expatriation", *The Delta*, 85). The expatriate's dream is overwhelmed with the sounds of natural rivers: "away from my hometown, I feel so missing / Dreams of fish slipping hooks sound like a hiccup" ("Day River", *The Delta*, 34)… In noisy cities, the old hometown became the place for people to remember and shelter themselves.

> Afternoons far from hometown, I hope the river to rise to the sky for me to see
> For my eyes are like two hollows on the river bank, where the goodies make their nests in rain water.
> ("Day River", *The Delta*, 34)

Day River, with its mighty and familiar surroundings, the wild but warm fields and the hard-working rural women… create a source of nostalgic inspiration.

Nguyen Quang Thieu's poetry is not without the anti-legendary discourses of the countryside. The countryside may be felt with the roughness that is embodied in images of dogs barking at midnight at the end of the horizon, wild wind breezing, and the moon being throwing "out of peace" and rushing "crazily into the clouds of motherland" ("My Dogs", *The Delta*, 71).

But above all, the countryside in Nguyen Quang Thieu's poetry is the space to preserve a wonderful childhood, a peaceful place for expatriates to come back after exhausting expatriation and a sacred place to purify and regenerate good values of life.

> There is a day neither sowing nor reap
> Escaping from the anxiety, returning to the field
> Dark brown soil emits the cool
> The rain everywhere is ecstatic in the late afternoon
> ("The Field", *The Delta*, 95)

When talking about the land, the water, Nguyen Quang Thieu emphasised the simple beauty of the river and the fields. Particularly, the inspiration for Chua village in Nguyen Quang Thieu's poetry always has a link between nature and woman.

> The women go down to the river for water
> Their hair knots break in torrents
> Down the backs of their soft wet shirts.
> They grip their shoulder poles with one hand;
> The other holds white clouds.
> ("The Women Carry River Water", *The Delta*, 115)

Vandana Shiva, an Indian eco-feminist, writes that the women "are laying the foundations for the recovery of the feminine principle in nature and society, and through it the recovery of the earth as sustainer and provider" (*Staying Alive*, 215). Nguyen Quang Thieu shows the special connection between the woman and nature by both realistic and romantic descriptions: the reality of hard living and the romanticism in the connection to nature. White clouds are reflected in the river, entering the woman's water, or they are the symbol of beauty that women always desire to reach.

In the nostalgia, the mother is the most important image - the reminder of childhood memories. The poet identifies Day river with his mother's hardworking life.

> Day River flows into my life
> As my mother with heavy bamboo frame goes into the rear gate
> I rub my face on her sweaty shirt back that is cool river at night
> ("Day River", *The Delta*, 34)

The mother and the river come together, exchange their roles and become a symbol of high spiritual values. These values are associated with a childhood paradise which never comes back in the endless future time:

> Day River, Day River... this afternoon I come back
> My mother is old like the sand on the bank
> Oh, the smell of dry sand, of my mother's hair
> I knelt, taking the sand on my face
> I cry
> The sand from my face flowed down the stream
> ("Day River", *The Delta*, 35)

Mother is like Day river with many variations of it. Broadly speaking, mother is nature and motherland. Ecologists have shown a dualistic table that is dominant: heaven / earth, soul / body, culture / nature, male / female, human beings / animals, spirit/ material, the white/ the colored...

The higher side is always "spirit", "rationality", "masculine" and the lower one "body", "emotion" and "feminine"[3]. From an ecofeminist perspective, Nguyen Quang Thieu's poetry contributes a voice to divinity in the dualistic relationship that this tendency of criticism declares: the male-female relationship. In memories of the child, the father is attached to principles and tough disciplines: "My father whipped a thread of soft smoke" ("Eleven Pieces of Feeling", II, *The Delta*, 51). For his mother, the father is the root of sadness: "Father brings the age of 20 on the boat and does not come back/ Mother stands burying her feet in the sand/ Sad tears are wet all the basin of river" ("The Laughter", *The Delta*, 37). And mother is still the same: wait, sacrifice and protect the children... With mother, the grown-up children are always young and innocent. Without mother, he is so lonely: he was covered by clouds and the darkness so much that he feels that all his footprints likely disappear:

> I clear the mother-lost yellow calf's footprints and it clear my ones
> When the darkness suddenly stop in front of me, I quickly go back looking for my own footprints
> Bust out crying
> I believe a witch has turned me into a calf
>   ("The October", *The Delta*, 43).

The poem is like the Mother's October premonition[4].

Nature and the women were appreciated as the origin and development of the world. In Nguyen Quang Thieu's poetry, these two images are in the center and knit themselves together. The girl in love is described by the majesty of heaven and earth: "The night has spread down the towel of love/ Your breath is aromatized with full of incense by grass/ Mountain winds cool your breast" ("One Love Song of Chua Village", *The Delta*, 44). Nguyen Quang Thieu does not write many love poems. And the love in Nguyen Quang Thieu's poetry is often regretful. However, the memories of love are always imagined in association with nature. We can be seen in Nguyen Quang Thieu's poetry many verses like that:

---

[3] View *Ecocriticism (The New Critical Idiom)* by Greg *Garrard* which was published by Routledge Press in 2004.

[4] Nguyen Quang Thieu wrote the poem entitled *The October* in 1991. 17 years later, his mother died on a day of late October.

> Day River! this afternoon I come back
> The fairy sails flew away
> You bring mulberry-colored lips over the water-absent river one day
> ("Day River", *The Delta*, 34)
>
> You swam in my hand like a fish
> Then leave me running into a lane without the moon
> As the fish escaped and ran down the mud
> ("Eleven Pieces of Feeling", VII, *The Delta*, 56)
>
> Your lie at night
> Like a lonely boat nestled in the sand
> ("The Boat", *The Delta*, 74)

Despite not directly depicted, the beauty, personalities and fates of people are expressed through the symbolic view: the woman is connected closely to the trees, rivers of the countryside. Nature becomes a kind of poetic signs.

It is one of the important ideas of ecological feminism that human beings and other species on earth are equal, connected and interrelated. This idea meets with Eastern ecological wisdom and is embodied in Nguyen Quang Thieu's poetry through the building of the equality between "me" and "others", between "human beings" and "things". The old hometown in Nguyen Quang Thieu's poetry is a person's warm childhood, his bitter departure and anxious return. There, everything is constantly moving along the cycle of life. Everything bears souls: of the congees, of the pottery-kilns, of the little dog, of the people, of the living things and of the native home. The native home becomes legendary, both individual and universal in the light of love and of faith:

> I sing, I sing my own songs about my old hometown
> In a porcelain container placed next to the pottery-kiln
> One day I will lie in it
> ...
> I wish my next life to be a small dog
> To guard sadness — valuables my old hometown
> ("The Song about my Old Hometown", *The Delta*, 87)

Conclusion

Born and brought up in Chua village by the River Day, a purely rural village in the North Delta, Nguyen Quang Thieu's life can be imagined as a depart-return journey. And so is his poetry career. So is his poetic path, it is a choice of going away from and then returning to the homeland. Experience of losing connections with the natural world caused by material advances leads to the dense occurrence of images of roads that lead to the city and back to the countryside in Nguyen Quang Thieu's ecological poems. In "The Preface" of *The Insomnia of Fire*, version 1, Nguyen Quang Thieu shared:

> When *The 17-Year-Old House* was composed, I saw my face and heard my voice clearly outside this volume of poems. Therefore, I continue writing *The Insomnia of Fire* a year later [...] I believe in my way and never refuse my own face and voice.
> (Nguyen Quang Thieu, *The Insomnia of Fire*, 5)

This thought helps the poet insist on an artistic choice. The works by Nguyen Quang Thieu marks a milestone in the way of innovating Vietnamese poetry. New text structures, new symbols and new poetic images help Thieu's poems step out of the same style and approach modern poetry alone. However, peel off the modern cover, and one discovers that Nguyen Quang Thieu's poetry is rooted very deeply into the tradition. In there, poetry reveals insecurity in the poor mental life when nature's beauty is disappearing and will continue *to disappear*. Far away from nature, losing nature, people lose both origin and homeland. Homeland becomes the sanctuary of the human's soul amid the changes of the times. The nostalgic consciousness in Nguyen Quang Thieu's poetry enables his "voice of special dialect" touch the identity of every human being in this life.

Works Cited

Bang, Jørgen Christian; Jørgen Døør. *Language, Ecology and Society A Dialectical Approach*. Ed. Sune Vork Steffensen; Joshua Nash. London: Continuum, 2007

Hubbell, J. Andrew. *Byron's Nature A Romantic Vision of Cultural Ecology*. Cham: Palgrave Macmillan, 2018.

Manes, Christopher, "Nature and Silence", *The Ecocriticism Reader: Landmarks in Literary Ecology*, eds. Cheryll Glotfelty, Harold Fromm. Athens, Georgia: University of Georgia Press, 1996. 15-30.

Nguyen, Quang Thieu, "Nguyen Binh's Poetry: A Key Word of Vietnamese' Soul", *The Literature and the Youth*, Volume 4, April 2018. 20-22.

Nguyen, Quang Thieu, *The Delta*, Hanoi, Writers' Association Publishing House, 2010.

Nguyen, Quang Thieu, *The Man Leaves the City*, Hanoi, Writers' Association Publishing House, 2012.

Nguyen, Quang Thieu, "The Preface", *The Insomnia of Fire*, Hanoi, Writers' Association Publishing House, 2015. 5-8.

Shiva, Vandana. *Staying Alive: Women Ecology and Development*. London: Zed Books, 1989.

Simon, Estok, "Partial Views: An Introduction to East Asian Ecocriticisms", *East Asian Ecocriticisms: A Critical Reader*, eds. Simon Estok and Won-Chung Kim, New York: Palgrave Macmillan, 2013. 1-13.

Thoreau, Henry David. *Walden*. London : Dent, 1995.

Thoreau, Henry David; Atkinson, Brooks; *Walden and Other Writings of Henry David Thoreau*, New York: Modern Library, 1959.

Thornber, Karen, *Ecoambiguity: Environmental Crises and East Asian Literatures*, Ann Arbor, MI: University of Michigan Press, 2012.

Chapter 6

Humorous revalorisation of traditional farming in some contemporary Vietnamese literary works

Hoang To Mai
Institute of Literature, Vietnam Academy of Social Sciences, Vietnam

Abstract

Hoya, written by Y Ban, is a work of satire about the subsidised period when Vietnam was poor and 'backward', typified by allegorical descriptions of old public toilets and their corollaries. Nguyen Huy Thiep's short story "Mr. Mong's story" depicts a market of excrement (mostly derived from old-style public toilets) under the management of a man named Mong. Although these two works exude humor, behind their naked wit there is an eco-subtext about the undeniable advantages of traditional farming (using organic fertiliser from human and animal waste, and vegetation) in stark contrast to modern farming that harms the environment. In re-reading *Hoya* and "Mr. Mong's story", we can recognise the rich and diverse eco-subtexts in these literary works that bring to mind the ecocritical concept of *dirt theory*. What is considered dirty becomes a complicated question whose answer refers to a conflict between outsider's and insider's perspectives or to an unstable relationship between nature and culture.

Keywords: dirt theory, dirt ambiguity, traditional farming, eco-subtext, human waste.

Ecocriticism as "environmentally oriented literature studies" (Thornber, 237), has been steadily emerging in Vietnam. Two books of ecocriticism have been published in recent years: (1) *Dry forests, shallow streams, poisonous seas ... and literature* (Nguyen Thi Tinh Thy 2017), and (2) *Man and nature in Vietnamese prose after 1975 from an ecological perspective* (Tran Thi Anh Nguyet and Le Luu Oanh 2016). Translations of ecocriticism are widely published in literary magazines. There is also a translated collection of international scholarly articles on ecocriticism entitled *What is ecocriticism?* (Hoang To Mai 2017). It seems that ecocriticism in Vietnam has developed proportionally to increasing environmental pollution, and it has attracted greater attention from readers and critics. There have been two international workshops on ecocriticism recently held in Vietnam: (1) *Ecocriticism: Local and Global Voices* (Vietnam Academy of Social Sciences, December 14, 2017), and (2) *Ecologies in Southeast Asian Literature: Histories, Myths and Societies* (Second Association of South-east Asian Nations (ASEAN) Ecocritical Workshop at University of Social Sciences and Humanities, Hanoi National University, January 26-27, 2018). This new critical movement has spurred the phenomenon of re-reading Vietnamese contemporary literary works from an ecological perspective. In Vietnam, no author has publicly stated that they are writing eco-literature, and there has yet to appear any major environmentally oriented writings such as *Silent Spring* (Rachael Carson) or *Oryx and Crake* (Margaret Atwood). But there are plenty of eco-subtexts in numerous literary works. In the process of writing these works, their authors did not seem intent on specifically creating environmentally friendly works, but some details therein can give readers the palpable feeling of anxiety over man-made damage to the natural world. Sometimes sustained and sometimes fleeting, these eco-subtexts can be discovered by a sustained critical reading through an environmental lens. Literary works with noticeable eco-consciousness on the part of their authors such as *The salt of the forest* (Nguyen Huy Thiep), *Giat market* (Nguyen Minh Chau), *The endless field* (Nguyen Thi Ngoc Tu), among others can be re-read from an ecological perspective. This paper proposes to re-read two other contemporary works — *Hoya* by Y Ban and "Mr. Mong's story" by Nguyen Huy Thiep — to explore their humorous revalorisation of traditional farming. Numerous details in these two short stories evoke the problems addressed by *dirt theory*. According to Heather Sullivan, this theory questions socio-cultural prejudices about dirt, or more accurately, the acts that are classified as hygienic violations in the community.

In *Dirt Theory and Material Ecocriticism*, Heather Sullivan states that when "green thinking" ignores "the less glamorous and less colourful components of dirt" in both the built environment and other landscapes, it "risks contributing to the dichotomy dividing our material surroundings into a place of "pure, clean nature" and the dirty human sphere" (515). She writes:

> I propose "dirt theory" as an antidote to nostalgic views rendering nature a far-away and "clean" site precisely in order to suggest that there is no ultimate boundary between us and nature. We are enmeshed within dirt in its many forms. (Sullivan 515).

The answer to the question of what is dirty and what is clean is not as simple if we pursue this line of thought because the answer points to conflicts between the outsider/insider perspectives. Tourists (outsiders) come to a pasture and feel uncomfortable when they smell cow dung, but the indigenous people (insiders) find it quite normal. Cowpats scattered over a field will decay and become a valuable source of organic fertilizer that helps the grasslands become more fertile, or ecologically speaking, they contribute to the equilibrium and stability of the ecosystem.

Sullivan distinguishes between *dirt* and *pollution*: "We must consciously construct a symbolic place in ecocriticism for dirt and pollution, an alias or icon that allows us to give dirt its due" (Sullivan 515). She argues that "there is no ultimate boundary between us and nature." Man, after all, is also an animal in the natural world, his body and the "dirt" associated with his body also belong to nature. And yet modern life has led us to forget the true nature of our body and allow ourselves to see nature as an instrumental object. We have thus neglected, ignored and even eliminated many of the gifts that nature has given to humanity. Coming back to *Hoya* by Y Ban and "Mr. Mong's story" by Nguyen Huy Thiep, there are some details in these works that refer to a prominent feature of traditional farming, namely the use of human and animal waste as fertilizer for crops. These details underscore the advantages of traditional farming in stark contrast to the harms inflicted by modern farming.

The first work to be reread is *Hoya*. At nearly seventy pages in length, *Hoya* is very close to an autobiographical account. It is not as well-known as some other works by Y Ban, such as *Letter to Mother Au Co, I am a woman, No gift for ugly Women*, just to name a few. Though her writing rarely receives critical praise, Y Ban is a darling of publishers in Vietnam, thanks to a natural and plain style that feels very true to life and quotidian speech. Most remarkable is her eccentric perspective, which comes across as very strange and absolutely independent, thereby leaving a strong impression on the readers. Grounded in *dirty aesthetics*, her works are full of naughty suggestiveness and haunting obsessions that often excite, amaze or shock the reader.

Written in the first-person account, the narrator recounts her childhood that took place during the war and the impoverished period of socialist subsidies. Such mundane events are not unfamiliar to readers who lived through the socialist period, but Y Ban's distinctive pen has transformed them into moments of eccentricity. The narrative in *Hoya* is rendered in a calm and measured voice similar to countless other autobiographical accounts. This measured and calm voice then recounts a series of very dramatic events that ensue. The author does not intend to recreate a nostalgic childhood. Most of the story deals with the narrator's obsession with poverty and the extraordinary adaptation of people to miserable living conditions. Her greatest obsession has to do with the filthy public toilets that stretch through her nomadic years of childhood. The homeless family of the little girl in the story has to go from house to house, so she has the "opportunity to experience" all the different kinds of toilets in the vicinity.

The first toilet is said to be "a latrine on a high mound with no covering. I did not know how people would go to the toilet on a rainy day, surely they had to hold it in until the rain stopped" (Y Ban 126). Subsequent toilets are described in even more humorous language and more melodramatic details. For example, the little girl recounts a very wild latrine at her uncle's house. It is a very spacious house with beautiful wooden furniture but no private toilet. Each time she and her cousins went to poo poo, we had to come to a river bank full of wild grass and snakes. At least two people must be there together. As one did it, the other one would stand watch. Every time they could relieve their bowels they were overjoyed. Once after coming back, all giddy they lay on the straw-matted floor and sang ourselves silly. But something very unexpected happened:

> Suddenly my brother exclaimed: What a stink! Who stepped on shit?
> We checked the feet and trousers of each other. At last, "the culprit" was found: my cousin with a piece of dry excrement on her impeccably white arm
> (Y Ban 129).

Perhaps nowadays the incident of excrement on "my cousin" will be considered an awful accident that invokes public disgust and shunning. But in *Hoya*, this is considered *normal*. In the impoverished and "backward" past, human waste, though stinking and unsightly, is nevertheless considered harmless and even useful to farmers. Y Ban's calm, matter-of-fact tone when describing incidents related to faeces is also a prominent feature, as it shows the author's sympathy with a life of deprivation and "backwardness" but also a life of rusticity and innocence. In this under-civilised life, things that belong to *dirty nature* will not be isolated and separated from nature, for they are quite normal in everyday life. Sometimes they are turned into jokes, like the scatological humour about what happens at public toilets. In *Hoya*, the author uses a whole chapter to talk about the public toilet. Having recounted numerous ironic incidents at public toilets, the protagonist thinks that such places would be "great for practicing the Vietnamese language." Upset at the pressing knocks from outside, a constipated man snapped: "Still at *it/eat*!" Thereupon a Westerner asks the man who just knocked: "What's he *eating* in there?"

Humorous revalorisation of traditional farming   77

In Chapter Four, Y Ban tries her best to fully describe the public toilets of a collective quarter for cadres who worked in a hospital. In 1972, when the narrator's father, a doctor, received orders to go to the front, her family was given a new apartment, which put an end to her nomadic days. The public toilet was attached to a septic tank. When newly built, it was pretty clean. Kids often sneaked out and brought books there to read for hours away from their parents. When children disappeared, their mothers would run out to the toilet and yell: "My God! Where do you shit? Hanoi or Haiphong?" But those nice days were quite short. First, the water was cut off. Lacking water even for personal needs, who could spare water for the toilet?

With a septic tank, excrement could not be swept away without water. As people used the toilet, the excrement piled up into a heap. However, as the rules of the dormitory must still be maintained, all the households took turns cleaning the toilet once every day. It would be clean to take a dump right after the cleanup. But "it's a matter of physical needs and not simply a machine" (Y Ban 175).

The second problem is the doors. They are gradually stolen. Most of the residents there are doctors, physicians and nurses, so they have to wear broad-brimmed hats to hide their faces when going to the toilet. It is the best way to reduce embarrassment. Last but not least is the cover of the septic tank. It is broken wide open; if not careful, you could fall down into the tank. The open-pit septic tank is a nightmare for older people. Even the narrator's father recounted a dream in which "he fell into the septic tank where excrement flooded to the chin." Then such a horrible accident involving the tank of excrement came to pass beyond the wildest imagination. Mrs. Mo, an old nurse, after burning up the used toilet papers she threw the smoldering ashes right into the tank. "Boom! A terrible bang, the excrement went splashing. As a result, Mrs. Mo got hit with a shit bomb from head to toe" (Y Ban 177). At the end of the story, having become a teacher later, the little girl of yesteryears goes back for a visit. The public toilet is still there. A few better-off households have built private toilets, but most of the others see no change in their lives.

Most readers can take the above details as unforgettable memories of the impoverished period of socialist subsidies. But these pages also raise issues related to the nature of the body. In the countryside, thanks to the spacious surroundings, each household may have its own latrine in the garden, and people will make full use of that natural waste for cultivation. In the city, it is very different. The old-style cramped quarters with public toilets make "going to the toilet" a nightmare. Here there is a violent collision between physical needs and cultural norms. Nobody knows since when "going to the toilet" has become a vulgar act. Humans are not "machines", for they also have the "physical" needs as other animals. This view questions socio-cultural prejudices about the natural in humans. After all, "excretion" and its waste are *normal* bodily functions just like eating, sleeping or breathing.

There are several reasons for which *Hoya* is not well-known. At nearly seventy pages, it is too long to publish in regular newspapers and magazines. Besides, its "disgusting" content makes editors flinch. However, upon close reading, some readers can see that *Hoya* is not only a work of uncanny satire but also one that contains an eco-subtext behind the façade of provocative satirical discourses. There are two details in the story that refer to traditional farming that has been considered backward for today.

The first instance is after praising the seductive beauty and fragrance of roses, the narrator immediately hears about the crude reason that makes roses bloom beautifully. The flowers that symbolise romantic love in fact only like night soil. A farmer tells the narrator: "If you want roses to get big and beautiful, fresh and fragrant, and to bloom in time, you have to feed them human excrement" (Y Ban 127).

The second instance is when the narrator describes her feelings when she contemplates the hoya in a neighbour's garden. She has never seen any hoya trellis that is as beautiful as that. "The verdant trellis is as big as a basket. Clusters of hoya are big and round like plates, slightly white, slightly pink, slightly green, slightly yellow, all aquiver. The flower is so beautiful that I stand speechless in contemplation and suddenly my tears overflow." But right after that emotional moment, the flower planter declares: "We must pay a price for any beauty" (Y Ban 190). To have such beautiful flowers, the planters burn used toilet paper and mix the ashes into the water, then pour it onto the roots of the tree.

Reading *Hoya*, we can see the author juxtaposing the elegant beside the vulgar. This narrative device creates a satiric voice that makes the journey to the end of the mundane world not exceeding the reader's endurance. It can also be considered the art of humorous contrast, common in satiric works. In *Hoya*, this device not only makes for cheery laughter but also makes the reader gain a fuzzy impression about the implicit value of human waste that has long been excluded from the civilised world.

The theme of the old-style public toilet and human waste is quite rare in modern Vietnamese prose. Perhaps apart from Y Ban, only one other author dares to try his hand at it, namely Nguyen Huy Thiep with "Mr. Mong's story". The narrator in this short story is also written from the first-person perspective. He is curious and wants to find out about a market for the selling and buying of excrement in the suburbs of Hanoi that only gathers at early hours in the morning. He gets to know the market manager there, whose name is Mong (having the same name as a device used for scooping up excrement in Vietnamese), and who plays the role of evaluating the quality of each crate of night soil. Mr. Mong does his job with pleasure and a willing spirit of disinterest. In this short story, we also see details that suggest traditional farming:

> The night soil market is held for about an hour from 3 a.m. to 4 a.m. right along the road to Son Tay province. This is a famous vegetable growing area. The egg-plant is very suitable for fresh excrement, especially human excrement.
> (Nguyen Huy Thiep 290).
> Pig manure is valuable because it is cool and can be used immediately. It can be applied to any crop plant. Chicken manure is valuable too but it is very strong, and only suited to the chilli plant
> (Nguyen Huy Thiep 290).

The experience of farming described above seems to be quite common everywhere in Vietnam's countryside. The author lists the effects of each type of fertiliser in minimalist sentences as if factually uttered by a farmer. In just a few short lines, the author has given the reason why the night soil market exists, and why there appears a character like Mr. Mong. In "Mr. Mong's story", once again we find that the events related to this stinky natural waste are considered *normal*. Nguyen Huy Thiep's humorous and naturalistic tone in this short story suggests a completely different view of the waste that is seen as a symbol of filth. It is a natural waste, a very useful material for traditional farming that is environmentally friendly.

In addition, in the characterisation of Mr. Mong, Nguyen Huy Thiep sends us an ecological message. As a Vietnamese master writer, he is the author of many wonderful short stories, but perhaps *Mr Mong's story* is the most eccentric. In a country profoundly influenced by Confucianism, the fact that a writer only focuses on depicting human excrement and its related matters is unprecedented. Mr Mong, the night soil market manager, is himself a very special character, full of grotesquery. He is about sixty years old, short, with a crew-cut hairstyle, big eyes, broad square jaw, brawny chest and solid limbs. He does not wear any face mask; there is absolutely no fear or disgust when touching and dealing with dirty crates of night soil and stinking tools. Mr. Mong's appearance, as well as his unusual behaviour, turn him into an eccentric in the eyes of ordinary people. But in the night soil market, he is like "a conductor who keeps tempo for the whole bizarre market" (Nguyen Huy Thiep 292). Mr. Mong does not sell and buy; he moves with alacrity and agility as he evaluates the quality of each night soil crate, joking around with his comments. For example, when a woman is so displeased with a low price quote she runs to him for help: "Mr. Mong, my shit is good like this but they say it is sour, how upsetting!" After some consideration, he opines: "It is good shit, not sour. Maybe this toilet is close to a place that makes tofu so it gets mixed with waste water from processing soybean." Then he continues with his judgment: "Your shit today is not thick as yesterday, it is very weak. Lower the price a little bit then!" Upon hearing another woman's complaint about the excessive weight of the crates of excrement he doesn't forget to lecture her: "Damn it for your greed! Who told you to pour water in it? You must drain off the water to make the excrement savory" (Nguyen Huy Thiep 293). The unusual vocation of Mr. Mong is explained by a rather dubious story. When he was a young soldier, he fell in love with an ethnic minority girl who brought him to the temple to make vows. He swore as follows: "If I am not faithful to you, then I must shovel shit all my life" (Nguyen Huy Thiep 296). After completing his military service, he returned home and married another girl, having forgotten all about the lover from his soldier's days. That is why spends his life around the night soil market because it is the price he has to pay for betraying his vow.

The stories related to Mr. Mong are very humorous, such as his special reverence toward that smelly commodity. City folk are horrified by the profession of collecting excrement, but to farmers such as Mr. Mong, it is an honest profession that brings many benefits. Sellers of excrement can make a profit, buyers of excrement hope for the production of delicious and nutritious agricultural products. In fact, the foul-smelling excrement is still safer than the nice-smelling but toxic artificial fertilizer. Animals never fear the smell of their stools and urine because from their strong survival instincts they know very well what is safe or harmful to life, and they use bodily excrement to mark territories. Humans are not like that, especially in modern times. *Dirt ambiguity has given them the illusion of cleanliness.* It is unfair to impute that a foul farm will produce unhygienic agricultural products because a squeaky-clean farm isn't sure to produce safe products. Farmers like Mr. Mong really grasp this. He thinks that the fertilizer business is "as noble as any other ones." He points out to the narrator a young man who deals in faeces in the market: "He could build a house and get a wife thanks to just faeces! Can't beat it!" At the end of the story he offers up a very humorous trade motto: "Neither mercenary nor sexy, the excrement business is the best in the world!" (Nguyen Huy Thiep 298).

Nguyen Huy Thiep does not exaggerate too much when letting his character sing the praises of this often-looked-down-upon profession. Collecting excrement is a profession that has been around for ages. It even received special respect from King Le Thanh Tong (1460-1497). The history books still record this amusing story. On the occasion of the new year, King Le Thanh Tong was traveling in plain-clothes disguise to observe the livelihood of the people. Everywhere he went, the king was overjoyed to see plenty of decorative parallel couplets praising his reign of peace and prosperity. But there was a house without lights, flowers or parallel couplets. Surprised, the king stopped in to inquire. The host replied: "To tell you the truth, my job is so abject that I dare not boast before anyone out of self-pity!" The king asked: "How could there be such an abject occupation?" "Indeed, I only collect ... human excrement for sale!" After hearing the answer, the king laughed and said: "Then yours is the most exalted of houses and glorious of professions. Your parallel couplet would also be the most excellent to put up. Why would you call yourself abject!" Then he called for paper and brush to write the following parallel couplet:

Wearing a pallium, I undertake the hard work of the world.
Drawing the sword, I gain complete sympathy from the masses.

The king compared the palm-leaf raincoat and the tool used for scooping up excrement (made of buffalo's bone) of the excrement collector to the pallium and sword of the honourable man. Apparently, King Le Thanh Tong valued highly the role of the farmer and all productive professions that nourish the people. Seeing the parallel couplet, astonished passers-by were quick to spread the word (Dang Viet Thuy 43).

Returning to *Mr Mong's story*, we can easily recognise the author's intentional juxtaposition of the city as a contrast to the backward countryside with the dirty and smelly night soil market. The market closes at dawn as the city, symbolising civilisation, begins a new day. The author even personifies the city, calling it "he", to describe it as a powerful and seductive man with lurking unpredictable dangers. In this work, the city begins to wake up like "a huge beast", like "a great giant" with a lot of worldly ambitions, with many bold dreams and hidden powers. "He is both slow and quick, drowsy and awake." (Nguyen Huy Thiep 295). People cannot predict "what his day will be, what he will do, whether he will start the feast of human flesh immediately or throw gold and silver generously everywhere like a King". A city is "something so much horror, so much fun and joy. There are so many wonderful scenes of paradise and torture in its many levels of hell!" (Nguyen Huy Thiep 295).

"City and countryside," "civilization and backwardness" have long become pairs of categorical oppositions, and from which the standards of civilisation are deeply rooted in our minds that most of us mistake them for something natural and innate. But in "Mr. Mong's story", there is a subtext that challenges these seemingly unshakeable precepts. Under the pen of Nguyen Huy Thiep, that very "unsanitary" market becomes lively and full of grotesque details, its filthiness gradually moving on to another aspect of the dirt, which is *dirty nature*, a questioning concept of ecocriticism according to Heather Sullivan, which is completely different from *polluted nature*, one of the greatest costs in the process of advancing civilisation. Actually, the dirt of nature is harmless to both humans and nature, as it has a reason to exist and can even become useful if people know how to take advantage of it.

It can be seen that the topic of "human waste" is very rare in Vietnamese prose. Perhaps only Y Ban and Nguyen Huy Thiep dare to try their hand at it. However, it does appear in oral poetry for the purpose of humour.

> *We the Co Nhue[1] youth swear that*
> *With less than two crates [of faeces] we won't return home.*

Or

> *Loving her not for her wealth,*
> *Loving her for her house has a double-pit latrine.*

There are even anecdotes with unclear authenticity. A bomb is cut in half, then placed in a public toilet to encourage people to go pee in the right place then they use the urine to water vegetables. On the wall of the toilet are the following verses:

> *Hey, wherever you go,*
> *Come here to pee on Nixon's head.[2]*
> *Pour resentment over the enemy,*
> *Coming here to pee is much better than doing it outside.*

---

[1] Co Nhue is a suburban district famous for collecting stools in public toilets.

[2] Richard Milhous Nixon (January 9, 1913 — April 22, 1994) was the 37th President of the United States from 1969 until 1974. During the Vietnam-US War, he ordered the Xmas 1972 bombing campaign in northern Vietnam.

The famous satiric poet But Tre [Bamboo Pen] wrote not only oral poetry but also such unusual lines of verse:

The fields listen to his departure,
The rice plants welcome night soil, the gardens are filled with batatas.[3]

This kind of folk poetry was popular during the period of subsidies when old-style latrines had yet to be replaced by septic-tanked ones like today. Their content reveals the habit of using human waste to serve traditional farming. It is worth noting that the laughter in these verses as well as those in *Hoya* and "Mr. Mong's story" bear no ill will. Humour is usually directed towards a specific subject, being aimed at the faults and weaknesses of this subject. If the satiric author is tolerant of the subject, the laughter will be full of humanism. "The spirit of tolerance can soften the sarcasm and derision, but not so that the laughter becomes boring. Whether it is interesting or boring depends on the wit and intelligence of the humorous author" (Hoang Ngoc Hien 405).

The humanistic and intellectual humour in the aforementioned works refers to a concept commonly used in modern art criticism: *dirty aesthetics*. In fact, in the nineteenth century, Nietzsche came up with a notion ahead of his time that art could transform any experience into beauty. Lovers of modern art all know a very famous work of Marcel Duchamp (1887-1968) entitled *Fountain*, which is a porcelain urinal signed "R. Mutt" submitted in 1917 to the inaugural exhibition of the Society of Independent Artists, at The Grand Central Palace in New York. *Fountain* has been considered a milestone in twentieth-century art, when for the first time an object becomes an artwork by the artist's installation. It can be seen that dirty aesthetics was born to adapt to the rapid changes of modern art. Its content directly suggests the birth of a fairly close concept: *dirt theory*. Just like dirt aesthetics, this new theory was formulated to challenge prejudices about dirt, to distinguish the dirt that belongs to nature from the dirt formed by pollution. Containing human ecological values, this theory makes a really important contribution to the development of ecocriticism.

Dirt theory can envelop many of the ecological issues of the modern time. One of the modern problems is "the application of industrial methods to traditional harvest and husbandry" (Kerridge and Sammells

---

[3] These lines of verse are said to praise the talented and beloved General Nguyen Chi Thanh who was in charge of the Party's Agriculture Board in 1961 to help stabilize agricultural production in northern Vietnam.

533). In the traditional farm, the natural waste of the human body used to be considered a valuable fertiliser for farming. According to a common proverb in Vietnam: *first is water, second is excrement, third is diligence, fourth is seed.* But human waste is becoming increasingly belittled and even despised. Before their assimilation by Westerners, many Eskimos used urine to make the skin beautiful. They even put a bucket of urine in the house and live peacefully with its smell. In agricultural areas that are considered to be backward, human waste, such as faeces and urine, is a useful material for farming. But nowadays, when living conditions have changed all over the world, that waste is no longer needed and the old public toilets have become a symbol of dirt and grime. Traditional farming practices that stay close to nature have long been despised and belittled for their low productivity and inadequate hygiene in a modern world. The notions of dirt from a civilised society refer to an unstable clash between nature and culture. The more society develops, the more culture overruns nature, to the point that "nature is rapidly being gobbled up by culture" (Peter Barry 254). Richard Kerridge, in *Environmentalism and Ecocriticism*, writes: "In all this work, the priority is to find ways of removing the culture blockages that thwart effective action against environmental crisis" (Kerridge and Sammells 532). People who put too much faith in modern agriculture often bring about the misuse of chemical fertilisers and pesticides, which have caused serious damage to the natural environment.

The misuse of chemical fertilisers as well as pesticides and chemicals that stimulate growth and create visually pleasing products has made food more unsafe. Many people living in the city have come to grow their own vegetables to ensure the health of their family members. Many balconies and terraces now turn into organic vegetable gardens in private homes. While these people are proud of fresh green vegetable gardens in the city, many think that this is a very unstable sign of a modern society with its neglect of traditional farming and misuse of scientific achievements in farming. This instability is one of the reasons why readers can appreciate the substance of *Hoya* and "Mr. Mong's story". These two stories bring back memories of traditional farming, which is very safe and useful, although unjustly considered as "backward". By re-reading *Hoya* and "Mr. Mong's story" from an ecological perspective and more specifically with the application of *dirt theory*, we can recognise the eco-subtexts in these and other literary works to be very profound and diverse. After all, writers are human beings, and from an ecological perspective, human beings indeed relate to both culture and nature. We humans are more deeply associated with nature than we imagine in our physical life, survival instinct, weather sensitivity, sixth sense, and so on. Therefore, it is not hard to explain when the writer's sensitive intuition is quick to notice nature's injuries, which are most likely caused by man himself.

Work cited

Barry, Peter. *Beginning Theory: An Introduction to Literary and Cultural Theory*. Third edition. Manchester: Manchester University Press, 2009.

Đặng Việt Thủy, ed. "Vua Lê Thánh Tông vui Tết với dân" [King Le Thanh Tong welcomed the New Year with the people]. In *101 chuyện xưa tích cũ* [*101 Old Stories*]. Hanoi: Army Publisher, 2005.

Hoàng Ngọc Hiến. "Những ghi chú về hài hước" [Notes on comedy and humor]. In *Những tác phẩm chọn lọc* [*Selected Works*]. Hanoi: Vietnam Writers Association, 2008.

Hoàng Tố Mai, ed. *Phê bình sinh thái là gì?* [*What Is Ecocriticism?*]. Hanoi: Vietnam Writers Association, 2017.

Kerridge, Richard, and Neil Sammells. "Environmentalism and Ecocriticism." In *Writing the Environment: Ecocriticism and Literature*. Zed Books, 1998.

Mai Văn Quyền. "Nông nghiệp hóa hữu cơ hay hữu cơ hóa nông nghiệp" [Agriculturalization of the organic or the organicization of agriculture]. Web. 12 Feb. 2018.

Nguyễn Minh Châu. *Phiên chợ Giát* [*Giat Market*]. In *Complete works of Nguyen Minh Chau*. Hanoi: Literary Publisher, 2001.

Nguyễn Huy Thiệp. "Chuyện ông Móng" [Mr. Mong's Story]. In *Tướng về hưu* [*The General Retires*]. Hanoi: Culture and Information Publisher, 2011.

Nguyễn Huy Thiệp. *Muối của rừng* [*The Salt of the Forest*]. In *Tướng về hưu* [*The General Retires*]. Hanoi: Culture and Information Publisher, 2011.

Nguyễn Thị Tịnh Thy. *Rừng khô, suối cạn, biển độc... và văn chương* [*Dry forests, shallow streams, poisonous seas ... and literature*]. Hanoi: Social Sciences Publisher, 2017.

Nguyễn Thị Ngọc Tư. *Cánh đồng bất tận* [*The Endless Field*]. Ho Chi Minh: Youth Publisher, 2015

Sullivan, Heather. "Dirt Theory and Material Ecocriticism." *Interdisciplinary Studies in Literature and the Environment* (2012): 515—531.

Thornber, Karen. "Afterword: Ecocritical and Literary Futures." In Simon C. Estok and Won-Chung Kim, eds. *East Asian Ecocriticisms*. New York: Palgrave Macmillan, 2013. pp. 237—258. *link.springer.com*. Web. 18 Apr. 2018. Literatures, Cultures, and the Environment.

Trần Thị Ánh Nguyệt and Lê Lưu Oanh. *Con người và tự nhiên trong văn xuôi Việt Nam sau 1975 từ góc nhìn phê bình sinh thái* [*Man and nature in Vietnamese prose after 1975 from an ecological perspective*]. Hanoi: Education Publisher, 2016.

Y Ban. "Cẩm Cù" [Hoya]. In *Thần cây Đa và Tôi* [*The Spirit of the Banyan Tree and I*]. Hanoi: Vietnam Writers Association, 2005.

Y Ban. "Thư gửi mẹ Âu Cơ" [Letter to Mother Au Co], In *Người đàn bà có ma lực* [*Temptress*]. Hanoi: Vietnam Writers Association, 1993.

Y Ban. *I am đàn bà* [*I am a woman*], Hanoi: Women Publisher, 2007.

Y Ban. *Đàn bà xấu thì không có quà* [*No gift for ugly Women*]. Hanoi: Vietnam Writers Association, 2004.

Chapter 7

Environmental Losses of Urbanisation: Reading Eco-Narratives of Đỗ Phấn

Le Thi Huong Thuy,
Vietnam Institute of Literature, Vietnam

Abstract

Đỗ Phấn (1956-), a Vietnamese writer, is famous representing environmental losses that are caused in growing urbanisation in contemporary Vietnam. He is widely known among Vietnamese academics as a literary author of urban ecology, particularly, of Hanoi ecology. This paper, using literary analysis and context analysis, examines Đỗ Phấn's representation of environmental destruction and other potential ecological risks as consequences of urbanising processes in Vietnam. This paper demonstrates that Đỗ Phấn's ecological stories embody a deep sense of responsibility among Vietnamese intellectuals for the national project of urbanising existing cities and countryside areas and the resultant ecological issues. Moreover, the ways through which Đỗ Phấn's stories address Vietnamese public concerns over environmental costs and associated social problems that emerged during the Reform (1986) indicates the ongoing practical role of ecological literature in political and social lives of Vietnam.

Keywords: Đỗ Phấn, urbanisation, ecological wounds, nature and human beings.

Đỗ Phấn (1956-), a Vietnamese writer, is famous representing environmental losses that are caused in growing urbanisation in contemporary Vietnam. He is widely known among Vietnamese academics as a literary author of urban ecology, particularly, of Hanoi ecology. This paper, using literary analysis and context analysis, examines Đỗ Phấn's representation of environmental destruction and other potential ecological risks as consequences of urbanising processes in Vietnam. This paper demonstrates that Đỗ Phấn's ecological stories embody a deep sense of responsibility among Vietnamese intellectuals for the national project of urbanising existing cities and countryside areas and the resultant ecological issues. Moreover, the ways through which Đỗ Phấn's stories address Vietnamese public concerns over environmental costs and associated social problems that emerged during the Reform (1986) indicates the ongoing practical role of ecological literature in political and social lives of Vietnam.

Karen Thornber asserts that ecocriticism of the twenty-first century follows anthropological views, placing social dimensions in its central concern. Researchers now focus on the literature about city and industrialisation as well as issues of environmental justice and associated social problems (Thornber *Ecocriticism*, 229-50). In Vietnam, since the 1990s, urbanisation has begun to widely impact on social lives (Đào Ngọc Nghiêm). The process of industrialisation and modernisation has gradually changed the face of traditional cities ("Thực trạng đô thị hóa"). Urbanisation has also simultaneously affected literary styles. There are more and more writings on urban areas, emphasising dramatic changes in society and environment in the cities in the context of urbanisation (Đoàn Ánh Dương).

The writing career of Đỗ Phấn is dedicated to the theme of urbanisation; his works, regardless of their genres (short stories, novels, or literary essays), and regardless of their time of being produced (before the Reform or after the Reform), are filled with stories in and about cities. Đỗ Phấn is particularly interested in writing about human life in Hanoi. Images of people and landscape of the capital, where Đỗ Phấn was born and grew up, return constantly in works of many Vietnamese writers. Nevertheless, Đỗ Phấn's writing about Hanoi is unique in its metaphors and descriptions of ecological wounds that are brought about during and by the process of this rapidly modernising old city. Specifically, in Đỗ Phấn's works, urbanisation is described as an avoidable changing process that is termed as "betonization" or "cementification": on the surface of the city emerge a number of "straightening skyscrapers" that look "like giant ant nests". Moreover, as represented in the novel *Vắng mặt* [Absence], modernity appears as a force with which human displaces nature. As described, city-making characters and scientists in the novel come into an agreement of building a city on the river; and foreign companies are ready to invest money and provide their engineers and scientists for the project. As such, the novel's narrator demonstrates that projects of urbanising the city are blatant and arrogant in relation to nature. In other words, the idea of covering the river with a modern city is symbolic in the sense that it embodies human's ambition of development at the cost of nature's displacement and disappearance. Moreover, urbanisation is represented in novels of Đỗ Phấn in the image of green fields that gradually disappear, and business incubators appear abundantly in suburbs of the city. In these enterprises, big trees, natural leaves and branches of ancient trees are all trimmed and decorated to make the trees look neat: "On some trees, sprouts begun to proliferate at amputated body parts. These trees are about to be uplifted and brought to mansions of wealthy persons" (*Rụng xuống ngày hư ảo* 52).

1. Urbanisation and Ecological Impacts

In many works of Đỗ Phấn, urbanisation is also described as a destructive force. As written in *Rụng xuống ngày hư ảo* [Falling down into Unreal Days], there seems to be some collapse from the inside of the city, that is, natural landscapes and cultural values from ancient times are in danger of being eroded. The old villas from the French colonial era, which were once the ideal architectural spaces, become out of place. This colonial architecture was not, in origin, designed in the way that it can be applied with air conditioning because the surrounding landscape of the city was once very open, clean and clear and because sound of engines in the city was not loud enough to disturb and break the quietness of the houses that are lying under shadows of trees away from roads. Or in the novel *Vết gió* [Hints of Wind], the city in the process of ecological erosion is very obvious: "the land in the west of Hanoi change dramatically just in a few years" (206). In his works such as *Rụng xuống ngày hư, Chạy qua bóng tối* [Running through the dark shadow] and *Vết gió*, environmental pollution and noise pollution in Hanoi are depicted as a concrete reality: "noises stuffing his ears destructed his ability of visualizing the space around him, pulling him out of balance and making him feel like he was about to fall down". The characters in Đỗ Phấn's compositions are often obsessed with noises which they consider as "constant quantity". In addition to noise pollution is dust pollution: "big-size trucks, container trucks, and high-quality passenger cars rushed and released smoke", "trucks carrying sand are covered with cloth in a clumsy manner, scattering soil and dust over roads while running ... motorcyclists disappeared into the dust. All seem to turn into dust in an endless red bloodshot pipe." In these lines, the city is seen as a huge construction site.

The process of building new buildings and expanding cities has put green spaces in the city in danger of being narrowed. Thus, another ecological injury of betonising Hanoi that Đỗ Phấn aims at representing is the rapid disappearance of green spaces. The issue of losing green space in Hanoi has attracted concerns of Vietnamese policymakers. For example,

Phan Đăng Long, Vice-Chair of the Central Committee of Propaganda, in his book *Văn hóa lối sống đô thị Hà Nội từ năm 1986 đến nay* [urban lifestyle and culture in Hanoi since 1986] (2015), describes that green trees in the old town and old streets decreased gradually. There are still cases of cutting down trees, even ancient trees, for short-term economic interests. Green trees in new neighborhoods are mostly planted in gardens that are forgotten and not taken care of. The area of greenery is the most affected in the south and east of the inner city, most notably along the banks of the Red River from Hai Ba Trung district, to Hoan Kiem district, north of the West Lake (154). Such concerns seem to find their echoes in Đỗ Phấn 's novels with abundant literary descriptions about losses of trees in Hanoi. As described, trees of the city have been mercilessly destroyed for years. New construction works have uprooted old trees to occupy their spaces. Traditional peach villages, which once formed a memorable symbol of Hanoi, are also transforming into a grand construction site (Đỗ Phấn *Vắng mặt* [Absence]). In the novel *Rơi xuống ngày hư ảo*, the disappearance of green spaces is more visible due to the author's use of the rhetoric of comparisons and figurative images: new urban blocks are continuously emerging in areas which are once filled with rice fields; soil streets and fields of the countryside are made into solid cement streets. The fact that high-rise buildings are growing more and more means that green spaces are getting smaller and smaller: "There is no gap between buildings that is big enough to look at the green fields ... The fields are now just in movies" (Đỗ Phấn *Rơi xuống* 127); "desert buildings were covered with white dust; white dust on the leaves was sucking last bist of the leaves' energy" (*Rơi xuống* 352). In this novel, Đỗ Phấn compares images of people on city streets on their ways harking back to the countryside at the end of the day with porridge that is spreading over out of the porridge pot being overcooked. These images that represent vast changes signify public anxiety of the destructive force of unsustainable urban development.

Moreover, climate changes and global warming — an effect of the companies and group's projects of exploiting and occupying the land of the old city for high-buildings — have caused the green space in the city to be fatal. As described in the novel *Rơi xuống ngày hư ảo*, while old trees in the city are gradually dead, young trees are not able to grow up and even about to die because people dig up and spreading asphalt over land for foundations of buildings and of pavements. As portrayed, the city is expanding in terms of physical space, but urbanisation and renewal of the city have narrowed down the living space of the city citizens. Characters in the novel always have a sense of the claustrophobic and dusty space of Hanoi regardless of the city geographically expanding as propagandised on media: "West Lake becomes a very small part of the new city centre. Looking at a map of the expanded city, West Lake is just like a drop of dark blue ink on new textbook pages" (89). Additionally, careless projects of betonisation and city architecture planning cause a feeling of discomfort and of being confined in closed spaces: "the cramped road aches more when the embankment has been built almost vertically on its right side. Ceramic drawings on dyke bank are clumsy and meaningless, which makes the space along the dyke appear narrower and more confined" (284) Narratives about the unacceptable behaviours of modern humans towards trees bring out a sense of deep pain and loss: development of the city has made the green spaces more and more confined, leading to a dramatic ecological injury in the city.

Not only trees but also natural ecosystems of rivers and lakes in Hanoi are affected by urbanisation. In Đỗ Phấn 's novels, short stories and literary essays, images of water, such as the Red River and West Lake, appear several times. In the narratives of these bodies of water, there is an explicit revelation of apology towards increasing pollution that is caused by human ambition and modernity: The Red River banks are no longer long red sandy beaches; houses and hotels are crowded until the edge of the river. Global warming seems to shrink the river: it is dried up all year round. Water is no longer red as its name suggests:

> The water in the dry season reveals its bottom. The accretion on the river widens gently to reach the shore. Only wind stayed. It stayed there for thousand years ... The wind blows bloody alluvial dust of the center island of the river into an overwhelmingly giant figure (*Vết gió* 66).

In another paragraph of the novel, the narrator sees the city's "lung", and this lung is at risk of being attacked by developing cancer cells that are brought about by the invasion of chemical substances in food and in the air. The city is likely to acquire deadly diseases. In another paragraph of the novel, the narrator expresses concerns about water pollution in the city in his description about characters' ambition to implement the "heaven and earth shaking" project of replacing existing befouled water of the West Lake with purified water. The utopian project reveals a concrete reality that is West Lake, the widely-believed giant and natural air filter of Hanoi, is being seriously polluted; all plants and animals living in it are under threat: A test is done on mussels and snails in the lake, revealing that they all have lead levels exceeding the established criteria:

Some scientists both at home and abroad have invented a heaven and earth-shaking plant. They plan to replace the entire lake water. The plan was under intense debates over the years. In the end, the plan was still under debate and water of the West Lake was still polluted (*Vết gió* 228)

Đỗ Phấn's narratives appear to have their echoes in many studies that highlight rapid urbanisation reducing the area of natural streams and green spaces in the city. And in reality, such a project of changing the entire waters of the West Lake has been discussed among scientists, biologists, journalists, and city-makers in Vietnam since 2016 ("Hiến kế"). This reduction definitely leads to the loss of environment and natural resources and the loss of ecological balance of Hanoi (Labbé 1-40; Bousquet 30-45).

Traditional ecocritics that divide nature and culture (Bull and Garrad) might find it unfamiliar looking into eco-narratives of Đỗ Phấn, in which nature is associated with traditional cultural values. Specifically, planting trees, or in other words, growing green spaces is seen as a cultural tradition of people who once lived in Hanoi. In the novel *Dằng dặng triền sông mưa* [Long River Banks in Rain] and the novel *Vết gió*, narrators observe the extraordinary absence of trees in Tràng Tiền street, the former commercial centre of colonial Hanoi; this street in the past was once covered with trees whose origins are not in the tropical flora of Vietnam. Lifestyle changes toward modernity gradually ensure the disappearance of the tradition of taking care of forest orchids for the city's natural beauty: clusters of royal orchids and dragon-scale orchids do not have any buds and are hung under collapsing bamboo frames. These wild orchids have been sold in famous markets of Hanoi such as Bưởi market on Hoàng Hoa Thám street but no longer taken care of. Reconstructing the embellishment of ancient Hanoi's cultural beauty, Đỗ Phấn emphasises the oblivion of associated natural beauty of the land and the people of Hanoi under increasing urbanisation.

Đỗ Phấn's stories of various environmental wounds that have echoes in contemporary scientific and journalistic discourses of urbanising projects. Environmental impacts in Hanoi indicate the practical role of eco-narratives in revealing and attending societal issues. In a lecture about ecocriticism at the Literature Institute in Vietnam in 2011, Karen Thornber stated that literature has an important impact on understanding environmental changes in the process of urbanisation and industrialisation (Thornber "Afterward"). As a person growing up in Hanoi, Đỗ Phấn demonstrates his deep concern for the destruction of the living environment of humans and all other beings in the city that is associated with vital and forceful urbanisation. Human invasion of nature's living space results in the loss of fresh air and safe spaces for both humans and nonhumans. Urbanisation does not only threaten the natural environment but also threatens beings whose lives depend on that environment. As a consequence, the image of Hanoi as a city in the age of modern transformation is associated with the ecological and cultural struggle that forms the city's "urban wounds" or "ecological injuries" in Đỗ Phấn 's writing.

Urbanisation and the Breakdown of Harmony with Nature

As a part of East Asian culture, Vietnamese culture is believed to contain respect for nature; the existence of biodiversity in the city is seen to depend on the availability of natural spaces and territories and on the symbiotic relationship between humans and nature (Nguyễn Tịnh Thy; Bùi Thanh Truyền). In Đỗ Phấn's works, Hanoi appears as a city that was once very nature-friendly, it is a land in its natural state, ecologically balanced. As described, Hanoi is a water city filled with ponds and lakes; every year in the past, the red flow of the river was enough to cover the mudflats in its centre. Thousands of years ago, the river was a dangerously wild with vast trees and many beasts; it is the living space of snails and the resting place of swarms of cranes. Hanoi traditionally was harmonious with the natural world (*Vắng mặt*).

The overwhelming exploitation of natural spaces and resources for the city's modernity has inevitably led to a conflict between people and nature. In post-war Vietnamese literature, many eco-narratives of nature 'punishing' human beings have emerged due to overexploitation (Tran Ngoc Hieu and Dang Thai Ha). As presented in the novel *Vết gió*, ancient shade trees in the city are wrongly treated as invaders of the living spaces of humans. The Nacre tree is the first victim of this exploitatively pragmatic treatment: it is seen to occupy much space in the city; its wood does not have any uses; its hard nacre fruits are like golf balls, if they fall on heads, they can cause injury. Consequently, it is often cut off when the rainy season comes, which makes it "look silly as if the guy was cutting his hair in the shop running to the street laughing" (252). Other ancient trees in the city also have to buckle under human devastation. For example, "*sấu* trees [a species of dracontomelon duperreanum] are full of bumps like the shoulder of a cow being crucified" (255). Images of wounded trees suggest the implicit tensions of human beings with development and preserving the natural world. These tensions are more explicit in paragraphs in which Đỗ Phấn describes Hanoi as the world of prisons and tombs of wild creatures. Hanoi is considered the place where wild animals all over the country are brought in. This does not mean Hanoi is a new safe haven of these forest creatures: some animals and birds are raised as pets; some are raised for bone and gall extraction in medicine making; some are for feather clothes and jewellery; the rest for food. Many beautiful animals of the old botanical garden now appear in the form of exotic dishes in parties. "These animals include gongs, hemorrhoids, deer, period, crocodiles, snake pythons, foxes, wild boars, and porcupines" (*Rụng xuống ngày hư ảo* 147). Even the rare magpie that is "an extremely valuable gift of wild nature" becomes a so-called "special delicious meal" of the city. People "traded their angelic songs just for a meal" *(Dằng dặng triền sông mưa* 252). Here, urbanising Hanoians are not far from being "cannibal holocausts." These descriptions signify a breakdown of traditional mutual relations between nature and humans.

Characters in Đỗ Phấn's novels are constantly in states of loneliness, anxiety, and regret that are caused by the collapse of ecological balance and the disappearance of the natural world. In the novel *Vết gió*, the narrator describes incidents of clogged roads and where motor riders "moved step by step slower than the pedestrians" (284). What is left in Hanoi to become unique are rivers with disgustingly smelling black streams and lakes full of stinking rubbish (56). People are paying high costs for their irreverence towards the natural. Moreover, Đỗ Phấn points out that losing the harmonious relationship with nature creates in humans constant feelings of lack. As noted in administrative documents, the population in Hanoi is increasing: "From the early 1990s up to now, Hanoi's population has increased from 2,051,900 people (in 1990) to 3,216,700 people (in 2006)... As of December 31, 2013, Hanoi has 7,212,300 people" (Phan Đăng Long 80). In Đỗ Phấn's works, the increase in Hanoi's population forms a setting that highlights a paradoxical truth of increasing loneliness among the city citizenry: "Hanoi is such a very strange city. More facilities for the public are provided, the bigger the distance between human and human" (*Rụng xuống ngày hư ảo* 27). As portrayed, high-rise apartment buildings grow like mushrooms: the green space is getting smaller, and the people are living on high floors, which results in an increasing gap among human beings, forcing them into almost absolute loneliness. They are separate from the city below, and from the rest of the building above; they are isolated from even neighbors in the opposite apartment (*Vu vơ ở lưng chừng trời* [Getting lost in the middle of the sky]). An absurdity is that the more crowded the city is, the more people feel alone:

> The street is like a bag containing people who contain some silenced suffering. Sympathy has long since disappeared. Competing to move on becomes certain when riding on roads ... [Human beings] are as though a group of crowded ants, hitting heads of each other while moving (*Vết gió* 55)

The narrator of *Rụng xuống ngày hư ảo* experiences a paradox that urbanisation, the expansion, and the reconstruction of the city make life and death close in the sense that graveyards are filled with dozens of graves and stand publically at corners of some streets; "nowhere is the gap between living and dead people close like this" (18). As also told in the novel, people's ability to empathise is also fading: "People in the city seem to have lost the ability to look at each other in intimate and understanding manner" (*Vết gió* 54), "In the city, people look at each other in an indifferent manner. There is no sympathy among them" (*Rụng xuống ngày hư ảo* 80). Family life also collapses. The distance between the husband and wife, Tuan and Han in the novel *Vết gió* is getting bigger because they all sacrifice their time for projects in their companies which secure them a modern life. Noticeably, characters of Đỗ Phấn realise that the missing natural world has caused them constant frustration. As stated in the novel *Vết gió*, human beings are more stressed out and unhappy because they live in a suffocating space, where they find no place to relax and to escape from a harsh working environment. People live in a crowded and stuffy urban space, instead of living under natural moonlight, which is hindered by artificial electric lights.

> It seems that Ngan hasn't seen the moon for a long time. Moonlight no longer holds an important place in the aesthetics of the modern city. Houses are very dense, they leave dark air wells that people do not want to look up to the sky (216).

Here, readers encounter an ecological message, that humans cannot live happy lives without being in contact with nature; modernisation that destroys the environmental balance and natural worlds eventually will destroy human beings themselves.

The ecological message is more explicit in many works of Đỗ Phấn. Specifically, characters of his novels, exhausted by living in the modern city, express their desire to return to harmonious relations with nature, searching in it a salvation for their wounded souls. In other words, characters of Đỗ Phấn yearn for moments of being immersed in nature to find the balance in life: rice fields radiate a fresh fragrance; they leave their car, immersing themselves in that serene scent (*Rụng xuống ngày hư ảo*). The character Tuan (*Vết gió*) absorbs the lotus scent carried by the wind.

Here, it seems that pressure of the crowded, suffocating city has caused in people a thirst for natural worlds. The Elder Quảng in *Chảy qua bóng tối* [Flowing through the Darkness] craves for clean spaces that are filled with birds:

    The wind blows through young branches with a pungent smell of leaves help him recognize the rising height of the old phoenix tree. The sound of birds chirping on his head reminded him of the wide and high foliages of eagle trees and Celtis trees (93).

    Nature here plays the role of a character, not just as a mere setting of the novel. Natural objects such as birds and trees are essential for the novel to reveal the destructive nature of urbanisation. More importantly, nature in Đỗ Phấn novel is essential in saving humans' innate attachment to nature.

    Đỗ Phấn was born and raised in Hanoi. His childhood was spent at the old quarter of Hanoi, West Lake, and pristine cultural spaces of Hanoi. Đỗ Phấn has written about urban Hanoi with all the knowledge and cultural experience towards his beloved land. In other words, Đỗ Phấn's works show the city dwellers' aspiration for a harmonious natural space, an eco-city in which nature reconciles with human beings. Đỗ Phấn appears to share with the public his attention to the ecological issues that are associated with problematic urbanisation of Hanoi. His works also form critical questions addressing social and environmental instabilities in urbanising Hanoi. Thus, Đỗ Phấn 's work is not merely a depiction of an ecosystem, but a profound philosophy of city ecology.

    Human beings have been facing ecological risks such as global warming, greenhouse effects, and natural disasters. Biodiversity is under threat, leading to ecological imbalance. Đỗ Phấn's literary representations of ecological crisis and urbanisation in Hanoi contribute a voice to increasing literature about environmental issues in modern cities (Schliephake, Bennet and Teague, Vandana, Shiva. *Staying Alive*, Verderame, Michael, "The shape"). This potential contribution is once again explained by Karen Thornber as an ecological crisis that appears all over our planet; the environmental crisis urges people to rethink their lives and their responsibilities from the planetary reference system and time. Through cross-cultural analysis of literary writings that directly write about the destruction of the nonhuman environment, human beings will have a fresh insight into the biggest challenges they are facing (Thornbe *Ecocriticism*, 60).

Works Cited

Bennet, Michael và David W. Teague. *The Nature of Cities: Ecocriticism and Urban Environments*. Tucson: University of Arizona Press, cop, 1999.

Bousquet, Gisele. *Urbanization in Vietnam*. London: Routledge, 2018.

Buell, Lawrence. *The Environmental Imagination: Thoreau, Nature Writing, and the Formation of American Culture*. Cambridge, MA: Harvard University Press, 1995

Danielle Labbé; INRS-Urbanisation, culture et société. *Facing the urban transition in Hanoi : recent urban planning issues and initiatives*. Montréal : INRS-Urbanisation, culture et société, 2010.

Đào Ngọc Nghiêm. "Đô thị hoá khu vực ven đô TP Hà Nội và những thách thức đặt ra." *Tạp chí kiến trúc*, 17 May, 2017, https://www.tapchikientruc.com.vn/chuyen-muc/thi-hoa-khu-vuc-ven-tp-ha-noi-va-nhung-thach-thuc-dat-ra.html . Accessed 18 Oct. 2019

Đoàn Ánh Dương. Vấn đề đô thị trong văn chương Việt Nam đương đại. *Vanvn.net, 2 Jan. 2017, http://www.vanvn.net/ong-kinh-phe-binh/van-de-do-thi-trong-van-chuong-viet-nam-hien-dai/1010* . Accessed 19 Oct. 2018

Đỗ Phấn. *Rụng xuống ngày hư ảo*. Ho Chi Minh City: NXB Trẻ, 2015.

Đỗ Phấn. *Vết gió*. Ho Chi Minh City: NXB Trẻ, 2016.

Đỗ Phấn. *Vắng mặt* (Reprinted). Ho Chi Minh City: NXB Trẻ 2017.

Đỗ Phấn. *Dằng dặc triền sông mưa*. Ho Chi Minh City: NXB Trẻ , 2013

Đỗ Phấn. *Chảy qua bóng tối*. Ho Chi Minh City: NXB Trẻ, 2011.

Garrard, Greg. *Ecocriticism*. New York: Routledge, 2012.

"Hiến kế làm sạch nước Hồ Tây." *VOV.vn*, 7 Oct. 2016 , https://vov.vn/xa-hoi/hien-ke-lam-sach-nuoc-ho-tay-557685.vov. Accessed 19 Oct. 2018

Nguyễn Tịnh Thy. *Rừng khô, suối cạn, biển độc ... và văn chương*. Hà Nội: NXB Khoa học Xã hội, 2017

Bùi Thanh Truyền. "Dẫn vào phê bình sinh thái." *Phê bình sinh thái với văn xuôi Nam Bộ*. Ed. Bùi Thanh Truyền. Ho Chi Minh City: Nhà xuất bản văn hóa-văn nghệ, 2018: 9-88

Phan, Đăng Long. *Văn hóa lối sống đô thị Hà nội (từ năm 1986 đến nay)*. Hanoi: Nxb. Chính trị Quốc gia, 2015.

Schliephake, Christopher. "Re-mapping Ecocriticism: New Directions in Literary and Urban Ecology". *Ecozon@* Vol. 6, No. 1, 2015: 195-207

"Thực trạng đô thị hóa, phát triển đô thị & những yêu cầu cần đổi mới tại Việt Nam." *Cổng TTĐT Bộ XD*, 1 Jan. 2015, http://www.amc.edu.vn/vi/tin-tuc-su-kien/tin-xay-dung-va-do-thi/phat-trien-do-thi-nha-o-cong-so-va-thi-truong-bat-dong-san/2762-thuc-trang-do-thi-hoa-phat-trien-do-thi-nhung-yeu-cau-can-doi-moi-tai-viet-nam.html 14/1/2015. Accessed 20 Oct. 2018.

Thornber, Karen. "Afterword: Ecocritical and Literary Futures," in Simon Estok and Won-Chung Kim, eds., *East Asian Ecocriticisms: A Critical Reader* .New York: Macmillan, 2013: 229-50

Thornber, Karen: *Ecocriticism (Phê bình sinh thái)*. Archived Lecture at Institute of Literature, Vietnam. Hanoi: Viện Văn học, 2011

Tran Ngoc Hieu and Dang Thai Ha. "Listening to Nature. Rethinking the Past: A Reading of Representations of Forests and Rivers in Postwar Vietnamese Narratives". *Southeast Asian Ecocriticism: Theories, Practices, Prospects.* Ed. John Charles Ryan. Lanham, Maryland : Lexington Books, [2018]: 205-228.

Vandana, Shiva. *Staying Alive: Women, Ecology, and Development.* London: Zed Books, 1989.

Verderame, Michael. "The shape of ecocriticism to come." *New Directions in Ecocriticism,* Sept. 2010, https://www.ideals.illinois.edu/bitstream/handle/2142/25241/verderame_michael_markup3.htmlhttps://www.ideals.illinois.edu/bitstream/handle/2142/25241/verderame_michael_markup3.html. Accessed 20 Oct, 2019

Chapter 8

Imagining Vietnam from the War Years to Post-war Period in *Nhiệt đới gió mùa/ The tropical monsoon* by Lê Minh Khuê: Templates for Ecological Narrative and Beyond

Nguyen Thi Nhu Trang,
Vietnam National University, Vietnam

Abstract

This paper shows the presence of ecological narrative templates in the collection of short stories entitled *The tropical Monsoon* by Lê Minh Khuê. In this collection, the author uses the familiar ecological narrative templates of world literature in order to construct a particular Vietnamese one. I will point out the differences in using these familiar ecological narrative templates and the construction of Vietnamese ones based on Vietnamese thought concerning nature and the relationship between nature and humanity. The combination of these two types of narrative template in Lê Minh Khuê's stories contributed to making the image of Vietnam from the war years to postwar period, in which the author emphasises the extension of tragedy and hatred, and the efforts to obliterate these narrative elements in favour of peace and harmony in the life and soul of both the individual as well as the entire nation.

Keywords: Lê Minh Khuê, Ecological Narrative Templates, Imagining Vietnam, postwar Vietnam.

Introduction

Lê Minh Khuê is a contemporary Vietnamese author who has a reputation for writing short stories. She joined the resistance war against America when she was 15 years old. She witnessed the changes that happened in Vietnam throughout her life, such as the unification of Vietnam after the long war, called the "Doi moi", or Reform period. During the war, Lê Minh Khuê wrote about Vietnamese military efforts with romantic and heroic inspiration, conveying in her works the spirit of "the country [that] comes to the battle". She is famous for her collection of short stories entitled *The Distant Stars*. In the post-war period, Lê Minh Khuê, constantly haunted by the war, began to look back in order to explore the reality of a country which had stepped out of such a bloody conflict and describes an oriental nation which was changing in regard to the hopes and tragedies of everyday life. Vietnam, both in war and after, is therefore present at the same time in her short stories. For Lê Minh Khuê in particular, it was important to depict a Vietnam from the perspective of the post-war period. In an interview, the author expressed this narrative commitment, saying that "The post-war [period] is the most terrible" (Trần).

The tropical monsoon (2012) reflects this view. The piece is a collection of twelve short stories, only three of which describe the background of the war. The remainder narrates to the reader about post-war life. Many stories that are set in the post-war era, however, continue to tell of the fate, and often tragedy, that has been aroused in Vietnam since the war's conclusion. This collection has attracted the attention of many readers and critics since its appearance, but there currently exist only online introductions and reviews. Critics have focused on the author's views on both the nature and philosophy of war, the image of calm and tragic postwar life. The post-war life in the author's view is both a tragic extension of the war and a journey to eradicate it. Also, the post-war period is the time to think much about the nature and philosophy of war and its obsessive presence in human thought. There has been no attempt to approach Lê Minh Khuê's collection from the perspective of ecology in order to explain the writer's imagination about Vietnam both during the war and after. I would like to put forth the hypothesis that the cohesion of these short stories relates to the creation/construction of certain ecological narrative templates. It will be shown that Lê Minh Khuê used more familiar ecological narrative templates from other branches of literature and created Vietnamese narrative templates to connect them.

The term "narrative template" derives from Porter Abbott's concept of cultural masterplots: "There are some masterplots [...] that would appear to be universal: the quest, the story of revenge, seasonal myths of death and regeneration [...]. All national cultures have their masterplots, some of which are local variations on universal masterplots" (47). They constitute "the mythological structure of a society from which we derive comfort, and which it may be uncomfortable to dispute" (48). In this paper, I also use this term as mentioned by Heiser (2017): "like the standard margins and Times New Roman 12-point font in a Microsoft Word document template. It is not unchangeable, it may or may not be politically oppressive, and it may or may not be consciously used: but it's [...] the standard narrative pattern until it's challenged or modified" (7). Some of the ecological narrative templates in Lê Minh Khuê's short stories, which are analysed here, are closely related to the second meaning of this concept. The Vietnamese narrative templates are probably the connection between the two meanings just mentioned.

The ecological narrative template is shaped by environmental/ecological thought and writing. Their meanings sometimes change when they are adapted to new environmentalist arguments. One of the dominant templates in environmental thinking over the last two centuries is the degradation, destruction, or decline of nature under the impact of modern human societies. From this thinking, many versions of this template appeared. For example, such a template could be an idealized vision of the countryside that contrasts with the city, as the countryside is associated with ecological sustainability while the city is said to be the center of moral degeneration, corruption, and filth. Other versions of this template include the worship of wilderness, radiation, environmental toxins, and environmental threats. In the twentieth century, the narrative template of endangered and extinct species is the most widely used and produces many related versions of itself. According to Heiser (2017), this narrative connects to history and identity of a particular community and a broader understanding of species; templates concerning biodiversity relate to the stories of cultural identity and cultural issues (Heiser, 4-5). Heiser analysed one of the familiar twentieth-century narratives in relation to the template of biodiversity and extinction: the polar bear story and the global ecological crisis and climate change. The versions of this template are formed in a way that both maintains and changes the original. For example, Nissan's Leaf Advertising used the template of the polar bear and climate changes and in order to create a new one: the journey of the polar bear to hug humans right at their homes and the solution for the global ecological crisis. The bear is a victim of climate change and the global ecological crisis. However, walking to the south is a journey which is meant to find a solution for that crisis. The hug plays as a metaphor of reconciliation between humanity and nature. Another interesting example that Heiser analyses is the documentary *Qapirangajuq: Inuit Knowledge and Climate Change*. Here polar bears are no longer emphasized as victims of climate change. Rather, it is a symbol of the intrusion of "Southerners" — Europeans or white North Americans who come to communities and ecologies without a deep knowledge of them. From Heiser's suggestions, I would like to point out the analysis of narrative template in terms of cultural identity and cultural experiences. The return to culture and tradition will be emphasized but will not imply resistance to Western culture.

Combining Familiar Ecological Narratives with the Process of Extending Tragedies from the War Years to the Post-war Period

The tropical monsoon is not a collection of short stories that focus specifically on ecological or environmental issues. Lê Minh Khuê rather focuses on individual fate and the stories of war and everyday life. However, the appearance of the ecological narrative templates in her narration is the way to emphasise the voice of nature, the necessary presence of nature alongside human life. In addition, that appearance is also a way to emphasise the extension and transformation of the war and postwar tragedy in Vietnam.

By reading this collection, I found that there are five ecological narrative templates: 1. Facing harsh/deadly nature and a return to the wild (*The tropical monsoon* and *Living slowly*), 2. The idyllic village and natural disaster (*Fresh water* and *Alone*), 3. Transition from a familiar to a strange nature (*Uncompleted romance* and *Thinking around*), 4. Nature in the war and nature in the process of urbanisation (*Memorabilia*), 5. The growth of the tree and the destruction of nature (*The Camry 3.0*); there are only two short stories (*Cooking* and *The day is very long*) in which the ecological narrative template is absent. These ecological templates are quite popular in narrative forms (novel, film...) in many countries and cultural regions. In my analysis, I will point out their transformations in Lê Minh Khuê's works.

The first narrative template "facing harsh/deadly nature and a return to the wild" is made by the combination of two ecological templates. In both stories, *The tropical monsoon* and *Living slowly*, dead nature is associated with overly hot weather, bombs, blood, and hatred. In *The tropical monsoon*, Lê Minh Khuê emphasises the closeness of this nature to war trauma and tragedy. Nature in Quảng Trị where Hiếu and Phong, half-brothers with political and personal hatred and the face-to-face enemies in the same war, is less descriptive. Prior to Phong and Hiếu's confrontation, with Phong gorging Hiếu's eyes out, Lê Minh Khuê portrays an image of a dry Quảng Trị, with the sand dunes and the bare nature of artillery shells: "In the night in the middle of Huế and Quảng Trị, flares light the forest at the foot of the Trường Sơn range, below is the sand dunes with cactus, a species that do not need water. Sometimes, from the sea, the gunfire hisses with a loud noise and then explodes in unstable places" (Lê 41)[1]. Returning to wild nature in the stories by Lê Minh Khuê is a way for the characters to face guilt and hatred, to find reconciliation and good nature in themselves. In the short story *The tropical monsoon*, Hiếu takes revenge on Phong by jailing him in the wild North-West, no permitting him to die but forcing him to reside in loneliness, cold weather, and the wild. From his perspective, living in exile on the cold Northwest mountains, far away from people and ordinary life, Phong reflected on his crimes and freed himself from hatred. When crossing the "path of the dead soul" to the farthest and highest place, Phong is described by his prisoner friend as such: "his appearance is beautiful but his soul is rotten" (Lê 67). After six years in the North-West, Phong, the famous killer of the so-called "Puppet Army", discovers the goodness in his soul. The words of his prisoner friend seem to have confirmed that: "You have returned to the nature of goodness. The way you wait looks human. You are like a child waiting for your mother" (Lê 95). In *Living Slowly*, the wilderness is a place of detention for those who were formerly brave soldiers in the war but became corrupt in the post-war period. The wilderness is the space where they face and think about their sins. It also makes their visiting relatives come to understand the philosophy of life — to live with kindness and goodness. The combination of these two narrative templates in each short story emphasises the continuity of human tragedy from the war years to the post-war period, including the ability to neutralize the "crisis of hatred" within the environment.

In several other short stories, Lê Minh Khuê does not incorporate the two narrative templates of "facing harsh / deadly nature" and "returning to the wild", but instead uses a single narrative template "Facing a wild nature". Generally, in Vietnamese narrative, people seem to fear to face a wild nature. But the characters in Lê Minh Khuê's short stories do so willingly, owning up to a sin and attempting to atone. In particular, in *Vietnamese Rap*, the protagonist wants to directly confront sin in an attempt to preserve truth in society and abolish falsehood. Thus, narratives such as *On the dyke*, *Vietnamese Rap*, which comment on the daily life after the war connect with *The tropical monsoon* and *Living*

---

[1] All quotations in this paper from the collection of short stories *The tropical monsoon* by Lê Minh Khuê are my translations from Vietnamese.

slowly in philosophy: the individual placed in the harshest ecological context is able to find their own good, reifying the idea that nature has never been the enemy of man.

The "idyllic village" and "natural disaster" are popular ecological narrative templates across many different world cultures. One case in point is the Japanese idea of *satoyama*, the idyllic village beside the mountain, which has exerted a crucial influence on environmentalist thought. In *Fresh water* and *Alone,* Lê Minh Khuê combined two such narrative templates. In *Fresh water*, the idyllic village and natural disaster belong to the characters' past. The protagonists in *Fresh water*, Thanh and Bảo, live in a village. Bảo's parents died in a flash flood, encouraging Thanh' parents to adopt him. Thus they live together in a family like siblings; the memory of disaster made them stronger. After some years, Thanh and Bảo move to a city in order to learn and work together, all while daring to face the challenges of a new urban life. In *Alone*, the character Dư lives in a city with her father. When she was just a child, Dư's mother passed away. Her father and she, thereafter, felt lonely in other ways. When Dư discovered that her father had found a girlfriend, she became very sad and always wondered why her father needed a new girlfriend in his life. Also, she could not accept the fact that her father was falling in love again. In a whirlwind of emotions, she decided to move to the company branch in the highland to work for a short time. While there, she witnessed a terrible flash flood which struck her colleagues. Hiệp, one of her young colleagues, faces death. Only after such a transformative experience did she changes her mind about life and loneliness. In these narratives, Lê Minh Khuê does not explain the causes of "natural disaster" as we often find in the popular ecological narratives. The writer does mention floods — a natural disaster - which suddenly appear and take the lives of people. This is exemplified by Bảo, who becomes orphaned, painting him as a brave young man facing death. However, Lê Minh Khuê wanted to emphasise that the natural disaster which is catastrophic is not able to break the idyllic village because it is associated with the Vietnamese good. The natural disaster as a sudden event causes people to be more connected, in need to retain the goodness and to hold an "idyllic village" in their soul.

The journey from "the familiar to the strange nature" is also a popular narrative template in world literature. This template is always connected to the cultural masterplot of the quest, and in *Thinking around*, this template also utilizes this quest masterplot. However, in the Vietnamese literature this represents the quest for truth. In *Uncompleted romance*, the anonymous main character moves from a familiar to strange nature, meaning that once he moves from a familiar place to a strange place he realises his loneliness. Thus, he ultimately returns to his old space. At the end of this story "for many nights he stands here as a polar bear looking at a house" (Lê 179). This sentence is reminiscent of the Nissan commercial advertisement for one of its new products: the all-electric Leaf. As Heiser (2012) points out "Only this time it is not humans who go to hug trees, but an Arctic predator who goes on a journey to hug a human right at his home" (240). Heiser means that the polar bear in the Nissan advertisement goes on a journey from familiar space to strange space in order to "hug humans right at their homes. So the global crisis comes home to the suburbs — and also finds its solution there" (Heiser 13). The character in the story *Uncompleted romance* similarly moves from a familiar to a strange nature and subsequently returns, but could not find the solution to his error.

The fourth template is the combination of two narrative templates: "nature in war" and "nature in the process of urbanization". In *Memorabilia*, nature is destroyed by both war and urbanisation in different ways. If war destroys natural resources by bombs, urbanisation destroys nature with buildings and construction projects. As an entity that exists alongside nature, human beings are lost in the movement of history among the bombs and buildings. In this context, the protagonist in *Memorabilia*, an old man, wants to retain his bicycle as a keepsake, so that he would not suffer mental trauma. This short story, with its combination of two narrative templates, can be read as a parable of loneliness and human imbalance from the years of war up to urbanisation because if nature — the symbol of harmony and tranquillity - was destroyed, it meant that human beings would be lonely, without shelter.

The last ecological narrative template is the combination of a template of the growth of nature and a template of the destruction of nature. In the story *The Camry 3.0*, these two narrative templates connect with each other to shape the plot. Tuyền, the protagonist, lives in a countryside in which the process of the day to day changes of urbanization impacts both nature and the human lifestyle. Every day, he observes the germination of a seed and the growth of a tree. In his view, a tree represents peace and growth. Nevertheless, every day he similarly witnesses people cutting trees and building mineral baths, which he interprets as the destruction of nature. The protagonist then decides to move to the city, ultimately seeming hopeless living an urban life. The story implies by this that only nature can give him a peaceful, hopeful life. However, people do not find a peaceful place for themselves in both the village and the city, because in both places nature implies the goodness and harmony of each person with it, but in the city human beings are destroyed. Human mobility and the search for real nature are synonymous with the quest for happiness and peace.

Thus, the presence of these ecological narrative templates and a reading of Lê Minh Khuê's collection through them can reference a connection between war and ecological degradation. If the war in this collection context can be imagined as a reaction against the imperial drive in which there are overlapping hatreds among enemies, as well as among those who are blood relatives, then there is no connection between man and nature, and ecological degradation is also a war in which humans and nature are divided, in which humans are pushed out and lose their peaceful environment. Tran Ngoc Vuong, a Vietnamese researcher who focuses on Vietnamese culture and literature, asserted that the Vietnamese always live in the family relationship and in a kind of consanguinity which is always associated with the image of the dyke and rivers (Tran 165, 83). This means that, in essence, Vietnamese life is associated with wild nature and close relatives. While still attached to it, it means that ecological degradation and disaster are imagined as constituents of a war which breaks the relationships between people and nature. Thus, from war to post-war, the tragedy continues and will be extended. Does this collection offer a solution to remove the divide and crisis?

The Vietnamese Ecological Narrative Templates: Returning to Nature and Indigenous Culture to Neutralise Tragedy

As I have analysed, in the collection of short stories entitled *The tropical monsoon* there are many familiar ecological narrative templates. However, what makes this short story unique is that, as pointed out, Lê Minh Khuê revivified those narrative templates by improving and presenting in them new layers of meaning. On the other hand, it is very important that he has created a Vietnamese ecological narrative that renders the Vietnamese culture and mind as the dominant and meaningful template connecting the above-mentioned templates.

The ecological narrative template that covers all of the short stories is "tropical monsoon". Each of the aforementioned templates always combines two ecological narrative templates, which often contrast in their meanings. They create a complex and changeable narrative in meaning and strategy. As we know, the tropical monsoon is a type of climate; it has wet and dry seasons, and the weather is not stable even though the monsoon climate in general is very harsh. In addition, the tropical monsoon evokes images of romantic and pristine landscapes. Thus, the tropical monsoon represents the combination of the opposites: the pristine and the harsh. In the short story *The tropical monsoon*, Lê Minh Khuê partly explains the tropical monsoon region in some of his descriptions, such as when he says "the moisture from the sea always makes people upset and uncomfortable, people do not know where to take it out so they do it on each other. [...] The bare land [...] sometimes seems as fragile as smoke, which can be swept away by the blowing sea breeze" (Lê 93). Standing on tropical monsoon land, his character experienced both the smell of the sea, of salt, the heaviness of mud, the aftertaste of hatred and the voices of unjustified souls.

Thus, if the familiar narrative templates related to hatred, the template of "tropical monsoon" emphasises that hatred needs to be resolved so that people may become stronger and obtain inner harmony. And although the tropical monsoon climate causes people to conceive hatred, by facing the immensity of the tropical monsoon sea, all hatreds could be dissipated. One could imagine many possible journeys but, for the Vietnamese, the journey back to the nature of the tropical monsoon is necessary. It is the journey back to their origin. The ecological narrative templates in *The tropical monsoon* reflect the image of a Vietnam with many opposite states in both the war years and postwar period: hatred and reconciliation, peace and disaster, balance and unbalance... However, "tropical monsoon" reminds one of the meaning of the origin. Hence, in the complex and full of contradictions Vietnamese society, nature, and life, traditional values play a significant role. It could be said that in *The tropical monsoon*, the renunciation of hatred and the desire to retain traditional ethical values as an ecosystem in the Vietnamese spiritual and social life are the main ideas and inspirations.

Taking a view from deep ecology, *The tropical Monsoon* is also covered and connected by the ecological narrative template of indigenous the "three" religions. For every Vietnamese person, Vietnamese religions are made up of the combined influence of indigenous religion and the three main systems of belief (Confucianism, Buddhism, Taoism). There are two pillars in Vietnamese indigenous religion: the cult of heaven, which emphasises Trời (heaven) as the creator of everything, and ancestor veneration, which focuses on *hiếu* (respect/ filial piety). The indigenous religion is deeply ingrained in the Vietnamese mind. Therefore, the Vietnamese imagine the world from the combination of two realms: the natural and supernatural. The supernatural realm includes the following: heaven/sky, earth, genie, ghosts, demons, and souls of ancestors. The natural world contains the universe, stars, earth, and creatures of the earth. These two realms connect to each other because, in the Vietnamese mind, heaven is the source of creation and defence of the natural and supernatural world. Heaven governs human life - happiness or misfortune, life or death. Humanity is the link between the natural and the supernatural. Thus, the Vietnamese always imagine the world via the model 'heaven — human — earth', and aim for harmony: harmony in body, harmony in spirit, harmony between humans, and harmony on heaven and earth. The world in the Vietnamese mind is always a harmonious whole of pairs of categories: heaven and earth, river and mountain, life and death, day and night, husband and wife, father and mother. In other words, in Vietnamese indigenous religion, Yin-Yang harmony is emphasised. The Yin-Yang harmony and the role of heaven are the basis for an adaptability of the indigenous religion and the three religions. Both Confucianism and Taoism mention the category of Yin-Yang and emphasise the dominance of heaven. The Vietnamese always want to maintain harmony. To achieve harmony, they always set the world, the state, the family and the individual in a cohesion, believing in a transcendent order — they aim, in conjunction with heaven, to the wu-wei principle and the principle of $tâm^2$. By analysing the relationship between Confucianism and deep ecology, Mary Evelyn Tucker emphasised that harmony between nature and humanity is imagined as a "correlative thinking" which is at the heart of the Confucian worldview. Because "the great triad of Confucianism, namely, heaven, earth, and humans, signifies […] that humans can only attain their full humanity in relationship to both heaven and earth. This became a foundation for a cosmological ethical system of relationality applicable to spheres of family, society, politics, and nature" (Tucker 131).

In short, indigenous religions and Confucianism, Taoism, and Buddhism create in Vietnamese thinking a narrative template that is closely related to ecology: the harmony of Heaven — human — earth. In other words, it is the harmony of Yin and Yang. When this harmony is broken, the tragedy will come to human life, the balance of society and history will be broken, and the disasters will occur. This thought and this narrative template cover the entire collection of short stories by Lê Minh Khuê. War or postwar life with bombs, hatred, crime, greed, selfishness are factors that break the balance in each character's life: Hiếu and Phong (*The tropical Monsoon*), Tuyền (*The Camry 3.0*), Bảo (*Fresh water*), Phong (*Memorabilia*), Dư (*Alone*), Bản (*The day is very long*), Tường (*Living slowly*). Thus, the characters fall into tragedy, separated from the family which serves as the background to create the harmony of Yin and Yang, the harmony of Heaven - Earth - Human. For example, there is a horrible story about a

---

[2] It's very difficult to find an English word corresponds to the word 'tâm' in Vietnamese. The concept of 'tâm' in oriental thought is very complex. 'Tâm' maybe mind, heart, soul...

half-brother paying off grudges by gorging Hiếu's eyes out. Given the profound influence of harmony in the Vietnamese mindset, Lê Minh Khuê in her stories seems to suggest that solutions for the character to escape from the tragedy that lasted from the war years to the postwar period is to attain harmony and find the balance between yin and yang. By obtaining that harmony, the characters would gradually escape from hatred and find balance in their own soul. The synthesis of humanity and nature as "harmony", in a broad meaning, is a view of human nature, an emphasis that separation of humanity and nature is impossible. Thus, it relates to a sense of decentering the human, a philosophical view of human beings: the human essence is the complex mix of Yin-Yang, in a relationship with and in reference to nature.

The presence of these narrative templates does not imply resistance to Western culture. As Edward Said has said, they are "returns" to culture and tradition and relate to "multiculturalism and hybridity" (xiii). He also emphasises that "the contemporary global setting-overlapping territories, intertwined histories-was already prefigured and inscribed in the coincidences and convergences among geography, culture, and history" (48). The familiar Western templates are "encircled" and drawn into the minds of Vietnamese traditional thinking and culture. Lê Minh Khuê emphasises that in the Vietnamese thinking the obsession and tragedy of war and natural disasters is really terrible, but it always aims for a desire, a way to find harmony, especially that which comes with balance in the soul. War and ecological degradation are definitely never associated with balance or harmony; these factors break harmony, representing instead disaster and tragedy. In the post-war period, this kind of tragedy and warfare is never forgotten. The obsession about it makes people more aware that harmony is their aspiration. Thus, Western templates are not too foreign to Vietnamese thinking. And the Vietnamese narrative templates make *The tropical monsoon* the mysterious oriental color. In this collection, the writer always looks for the interpretation of history and life (in the past and the present) through the relationship between nature and Vietnamese thinking. War or natural disaster creates an imbalance in history and life. Nature is the factor that evokes that history, life needs to release the main imbalance in nature, in the relation of nature and human, of the yin and yang. This view has a distinctively Vietnamese color, but in a broader view, it partly reflects a kind of global ecological thinking that emphasises the anthropogenic crisis.

Conclusion

The short stories in the collection entitled The tropical monsoon by Lê Minh Khuê are simple and brief. However, they draw paintings by using many colors of history and life, past and present. Through the narrative templates in the short stories, the reader would image a Vietnam with respect to the tragedies of war and postwar life, a changed and constantly changing Vietnam, a Vietnam of many opposing states, and a Vietnam which finds solutions to the complex problems of the past and present history in its own cultural background and national identity. Coming back and facing the true nature of the tropical monsoon, that is, returning to the harmony of Heaven — Earth — Human, of Yin and Yang, is the way out of the tragedy in order to find peace for each person. This is probably Lê Minh Khuê's suggestion through ecological narrative templates in the collection of her short stories.

Work Cited

Abbott, Porter. *The Cambridge Introduction to Narrative.* Cambridge University Press, 2008.

Heise, Ursula K. *Imagining Extinction: The cultural meanings of Endangered species.* The University of Chicago Press, Chicago and London, 2016.

Heiser, Ursula K. *Narrative, Ecocriticism, and the Environmental Humanities.* Lecture in University of Social Sciences and Humanities, VNU, Hanoi, December 2017.

Lê, Minh Khuê. *Nhiệt đới gió mùa* [*The tropical monsoon*]. Publishing House of Writers Association and Nhã Nam, Hanoi, 2012.

Said, Edward W. *Culture and Imperialism.* Vintage Book, A Division of Random House, Inc., New York, 1994.

Trần, Hoàng Thiên Kim. "Nhà văn Lê Minh Khuê: Thấu hiểu nỗi bất an của đời sống" [Lê Minh Khuê: Understanding the insecurity of life]. *An ninh thế giới online,* 12 Feb. 2017, antg.cand.com.vn/Kinh-te-Van-hoa-The-Thao/Nha-van-Le-Minh-Khue-Thau-hieu-noi-bat-an-cua-doi-song-427595/. Access 9 June 2018.

Trần, Ngọc Vương. *Thực thể Việt: Nhìn từ các tọa độ chữ* [Vietnamese entity: a view from the word coordinates]. Publisher Knowledge, Hanoi, 2010.

Tucker, Mary Evelyn. "Confucianism and Deep Ecology". *Deep Ecology and World Religions New Essays on Sacred Grounds,* edited by David Landis Barnhill and Roger S. Gottlieb, State University of New York Press, 2001, pp. 127-52.

Chapter 9

Nature and Humans in Sino-Vietnamese conceptions and practices. Articulations between Asian vernacular "analogism" and Western modern "naturalism" ontologies

Christian Culas,
French National Center for Scientific Research (CNRS),
Centre Norbert Elias, EHESS, France

Abstract

There are very few conceptions of what nature is in Vietnam, and of what constitutes relations between humans and non-humans. My main objective is to describe and to understand what the conceptions and practices of nature are in Vietnam today. To attempt to reconstruct the conceptions of the world and the relationships humans/nature, or the "non human" (Latour 2004), in Vietnam, I will proceed in two ways. First, I will give an overview of the history of the relations between human/nature and human/human (politics), as Vietnam is one important place where the traditional Chinese mode of identification and worldview ("analogism" Descola 2005) and modern Western mode of identification and worldview meet ("naturalism"). Thus, a new synthetic and hybrid way of thought and action is formed with these interactions. Second, some examples of what nature means in Sino-Vietnamese conceptions and practices will show the diversity of ways of thinking about nature. Historical processes that built the current conceptions and practices of nature in Vietnam are deeply syncretic and hybrid.

Three examples will help us to understand the diversity of Vietnamese conceptions of nature: a) Taoist conceptions of Nature where man can learn and experience nature through practice, b) Man can integrate some powers of nature by eating them, and c) In Vietnamese conceptions and actions, nature can be built by and around the human in a "nature garden", similar to Japanese landscapes called *"Satoyama"* where biodiversity is built and maintained by humans.

These examples of contextualised conceptions and actions with nature can show how the analogical tradition can articulate, integrate with, and oppose different forms of naturalism in certain specific situations to build the current conceptions and practices of nature in Vietnam.

Keywords: Vietnam, China, Nature, relation human non-human, Analogism/Naturalism.

Introduction

1) Findings

According to surveys I conducted since 2006 in North and South Vietnam[1] and on the basis of the literature, we find that the vast majority of projects for the protection of natural areas or the environment in general applied in Vietnam have failed to yield favourable results.. (O'Rourke, 1995, 2001 ; Zink 2013).

There are multiple reasons for these failures. Some are related to Vietnamese public policies. Vietnam, like many other countries[2], faces a dilemma in its development process. In order to maintain a high rate of economic growth, Vietnamese governments have chosen to promote industrialisation and intensive agriculture at the expense of protecting the environment. (Bass et al.; O'Rourke; Sikor and O'Rourke). Other reasons are also related to the functioning of the information-communication systems and control of violations of environmental protection laws. In short, the complexity of the laws and the very frequent corruption among civil servants are obvious obstacles to effective protection (Do; Culas forthcoming).

Based on field studies and a wide range of literature on this topic, there is one reason that is usually forgotten or missing by researchers and experts: It

---

[1] Lao Cai and Kien Giang provinces.

[2] See extreme pollution cases of Chinese cities.

is about the ways of thinking about the relations between humans and nature by the Vietnamese population.

My paper focuses on some of the specificities of nature's conceptions and practices in Vietnam in order to better understand the difficulties of applying environmental protection projects in this country. It is interesting to note that all the environmental protection projects in Vietnam have been conceived and designed on a Western philosophical and ontological reference. Implicitly, the populations involved locally in these projects are supposed to have the same conceptions of nature as Westerners.

However, there is a need to explain what "Western philosophical and ontological reference" means. Historical and philosophical research on the construction of the idea of "nature" in the West has shown that the exclusive division between humans (culture, language, thought) and nature (without culture, without language, without thought) is a product from the Renaissance (14th to 16th centuries) and the beginnings of modern science in Europe (Descola; Latour). In short, from this period, we observe a formalisation of the thought of nature according to a dualistic framework: Culture / Nature, Human / Non-human. This ontological schema or "modes of identification" developed in the West to think about nature is called "naturalism" because it essentialises nature as an entity distinct from humans. While in China, Vietnam and Japan, even though the division of Nature / Culture exists, it is less rigid and there are various ways that connect humans and non-humans by correspondence and analogies (Bruun and Kalland).

The central idea of this approach is that each culture, each human group or society will classify humans and non-humans[3] according to a large number of criteria (same physical, same ancestors, same kinship system, same spirit, etc.). This broad set of criteria can be summarised into two main distinctions: resemblance / difference of interiority (spirit) and resemblance / difference of physicalities (body). The synthesis of these ontological possibilities is presented in the diagram below.

---

[3] Since B. Latour (2004), we prefer the notion of "non-human", which is more descriptive and not ideological than "nature", because the opposition between human and nature is not necessary. The non-human can be an object (a mountain, a river, a car ...), a living being (plant, animal), an arrangement or a spirit or a god.

	Modes of identification	Modes of identification	
- Resemblance of interiority (spirit) - Difference of physicalities (body)	**Animism** (South America, North America, Siberia…)	**Totemism** (Australia, Africa…)	- Resemblance of interiority (spirit) - Resemblance of physicalities (body)
- Difference of interiority (spirit) - Resemblance of physicalities (body)	**Naturalism** (Western countries…)	**Analogism** (China, Vietnam, Japan, India, South America…)	Difference of interiority (spirit) - Difference of physicalities (body)

Fig. 10.1 Scheme of modes of identification possible (Descola 221, adapted by Culas)

The above-mentioned theoretical framework will be the basis of my argument. The thinking and practice of Chinese and Vietnamese people in relation to nature are globally classified in the "analogism" category because, in this mode, relations between humans and non-humans are such that "[e]verything is constantly connected with everything". The differences between humans and non-humans are not key to such thinking in Sino-Vietnamese conceptions. As such, all the categories of actors in the world (human and non-human) are different, thus the Chinese and Vietnamese modes of identification work on the mapping of these different categories, or what is called as "analogism". It is by analogy that the different categories of the world are strongly linked to make sense of the world around us.

But for this diversified world to be comprehensible, these analogical modes of identification have created many forms of hierarchies between beings. The first of them applies to the cosmos which is divided into three levels: the highest is the "Sky", the middle level is that of "Men" and the lower level that of the "Earth". The classic Chinese formula is "Put the man in the center" (以人为本) » (Ouyang 1). In the same logic, China, Vietnam and Japan, have built social and linguistic hierarchies between men. As evidenced by the different levels of Vietnamese terms, the use of neutral "I" and "you" (as in English) is most often replaced by classificatory terms such as "older brother", "younger brother", "older aunt", "younger aunt", etc. In these systems of thought, the person is not isolated by the words that designate her, to name a person is to call to the all social, cultural and symbolic hierarchies that give the person his or her complete position and status (Berque; Mus).

2) State of art about Vietnam

The questions we raise here about the thought and actions of and about nature have been analysed in different ways for a long time in China[4] and Japan[5], but they are still understudied, and there is no intellectual engagement in Vietnam about the relationship between human and nature.

I would like to start with a brief outline of the ideas in the literature on the relationships between humans and non-humans in Vietnam. Unlike China and Japan where there are philosophical and religious schools that study the relationship between men and nature for several centuries, the first works on the question of nature in Vietnam dated from the French colonial period[6] (1858-1945) (Przyluski, Cadière; Stein). These are usually ethnographic studies of pagoda gardens and tree cults. In the years 1980 to 2000 with the economic liberalization of the country, new studies deal with these topics. The most remarkable works based on precise field surveys are those of ethnobotanist Dinh Trong Hieu[7]. Two of his articles directly address broader issues such as "The Impacts of the Communist or Marxist-Leninist Development Model on the Environment in Vietnam" (1990) and "The Relationship between the Social Sciences and Biodiversity" (2003).

For the year 2000, we note an original sociological survey through a questionnaire conducted on twenty people in Hanoi (Pham and Rambo 2003). The main objective of this innovative study was "Comparative studies of public perceptions of environmental problems and environmental consciousness in Hong Kong, Japan, Thailand, and Vietnam". The secondary objectives were to know how people perceive environmental responsibilities between individuals, governments and large private companies. The main

---

[4] For example, in China, the study of relationships human / nature is very old, as shown by a poet and philosopher, Tao Yuanming (365-427) which is a symbol of classical Chinese study about nature (Lu 2017; Lee 2005)

[5] Japan concentrates several original initiatives. The most important is certainly "International Partnership for the Satoyama Initiative" promoting collaboration in the conservation and restoration of sustainable human-influenced natural environments (Socio-Ecological Production Landscapes and Seascapes) through broader global recognition of their value (http://satoyama-initiative.org/). Note also the projects from Research Institute for Humanity and Nature (Kyoto, 2001) to conduct integrated researches in global environmental studies. (Batten and Brown 2015; Kazuhiko 2010; Iwatsuki 2008).

[6] Dinh T. H. (1996-1997)

[7] Researcher at French National Center for Scientific Research, Museum of Natural History (Paris) from 1981 to 2003.

weakness of this survey was that it only records responses to an environmental questionnaire. This is not enough to know the real practices of the Vietnamese people.

We must also point out Frédéric Thomas's Ph.D. thesis about *The forest exposed: anthropological essay on the construction of a tropical scientific object: "Indochinese forests and woods"*, (2003). From a historical point of view, several chapters approach the Chinese and Vietnamese cosmologies on forests and on nature and also introduce the diversity of conceptions of nature in Vietnam by highlighting the cosmologies and rites of certain ethnic groups of Highland of Central Vietnam.

Except for Dinh Trong Hieu's works, there is to my knowledge no serious field study that deals with the relationship of men to nature among Kinh (a major ethnic group in Vietnam). On the other hand, some anthropologists specialising in "minority" mountain ethnic groups have studied the relationships between local cosmologies and the conceptions of nature[8]. With regards to the literature on Vietnam, there is a lack of both field research and synthetic and philosophical approaches that integrate the symbolic and phenomenological dimensions of the man / nature relationships.

However, from the above data and their contextualisation with the religious and popular representations of the Vietnamese, it is possible to begin to see the outlines of the thoughts and practices of nature. Of course, there are many studies in Vietnam on the management of natural resources[9] (fauna, flora, management of protected areas) but this research is almost always focused on a "Western naturalism" approach and is based on the principle that man and nature are two exclusive and distinct entities. On the other hand, almost all of these works study human and natural relations through the relations of uses, productive relations and technical relations. All symbolic, religious, emotional and philosophical dimensions of human / nature relationships are forgotten. The purpose of this paper is also to show that in order to understand what nature means in Vietnam today, we must be able to integrate both the technical and scientific dimensions (such as the utilitarian uses of natural resources) as well as the dimensions less easy to grasp and to describe, such as those related to tree cults, sacred forests or the symbolic aspects of plants and animals of traditional Vietnamese medicine. In this way, my approach is similar with Augustin Berque (2014)

---

[8] Dournes (1954, 1974), Nguyen Van Thang (1995) and Vuong Xuan Tinh (1998).

[9] Vu and Nguyen (2011), USAID (2013)

Nature and Humans   117

when he finds that modern science based on the "naturalist" modes of identification focuses solely on the technical, utilitarian and economic dimensions of human activities, but that it obscures all the activities of "phenomenological" type that can also be called sensitive, emotional, affective or belief-related activities.

To attempt to reconstruct the conceptions of the world and the relationships humans / nature in Vietnam, I will proceed in two ways that will structure this article:

First, I will give an overview of historical landmarks of the conceptions of relations human/nature and human/human (politics), because Vietnam is one important place where traditional Chinese modes of identification and modern Western modes of identification meet and build a new synthetic way of thought and action.

Second, some examples of what nature means in Sino-Vietnamese conceptions will show the diversity of ways of thinking and acting nature. What I present today is still a work in progress, and this is just the first step of a long-term research project.

I - Historical landmarks of the conceptions of relations human/non-human

Presenting the history of the conceptions of nature in Vietnam in a few broad phases may seem very simplistic, it is not a question here of going into details but rather of showing how historical conceptions and modes of identification can be synthesised to constitute the complexity of current conceptions.

DATE	Ca 3000 BCE - 111 BCE	ca. 111 BCE - 939 CE	939 CE - 1862	1862 - 1945	1945 - 1986	1986 -> today
Political System	...Dong Son culture - Nan Yueh kingdon	China's Han conquers Nan Yueh	Vietnamese dynasties	French colonisation in Vietnam	First communist period	Second transitional communist period
Modes of identification	Indigenous Vietnamese mode of identification	Introduction of Chinese analogical mode of identification	Syncretism between Vietnamese and Chinese modes of identification	Introduction of French naturalist mode of identification	Development of Marxist-Leninist naturalist mode of identification	Development of "Market economy" mode of identification

Fig. 10.2. Chronology of ontological conceptions in Vietnam (Culas 2018)

I will only outline the four bold steps in the diagram above, as they are the most important milestones in the evolution of human and non-human relationship conceptions in Vietnam.

1) Ancient Vietnam under Chinese rule

From the 1st century BCE to the 10th century CE, Vietnam was under Chinese rule. During this long colonization, intellectual and political elites were trained according to Chinese criteria to build a body of scholars. This body of political, moral and aesthetic principles would then gradually spread to the entire Vietnamese population. Thus these principles and their practical applications would be borrowed, assimilated and often adapted by the population of all social classes. Thus, there was an established Sino-Vietnamese cosmology without conceptual separation between nature and human. Some Chinese literary formulas describe this cosmology as: "All belong to The Great All, the orders and hierarchies create the links between them". For example, the conception of imperial political power is directly connected to the cosmological conception of the world. The Chinese character "King" 王 (Váng) has a traditional etymology: three horizontal lines are Sky, Human and Earth, and the vertical line is making the best connection between them. Its symbolic meaning is "To govern is to establish the harmony between Heaven, Human and the Earth". We find again the idea of the link and the search for harmony between entities and distinct cosmological spaces. Relationships between human and nature and human and human are based on an analogical mode of identification (Descola).

2) French colonisation (1858-1945)

French colonisation (1858-1945) introduced in Vietnam a conceptual and exclusive separation between nature and humans[10]. The two domains that will have the greatest impact in Vietnamese thinking are the introduction of modern scientific, technical and industrial approaches and, some new political ideas including individualism, the State-Nation system, democratic and human rights. We note that the Vietnamese elite incorporated some elements of Western naturalism with a strong focus on political points of view because their main objective was national emancipation in reaction to colonial domination. But they paid less attention to the new conception of nature. But the most important borrowed items about relationships with nature are probably Western medicine and science. Today we can observe a juxtaposition without contact of two medical systems in Vietnam: the traditional one based on an ancient knowledge fund partly common to China, the other Western-style scientific and technical medicine. Western naturalism mode of identification was also a strong basis for Marxist-Leninist ideology.

The liberation of the country from the French colonial forces will be partly thanks to communist organisations. I will distinguish two communist periods because their political orientations and practical applications are very different.

3) First Communist Period (1945 à 1986)

During the First Communist Period (1945 à 1986), Marxist-Leninist ideology and project was an imported system of human relationships from Russia, China and France. In short, we can say this is an extreme case of application of Western naturalism (Descola) because the development of human society can be done without paying attention to non-humans. The main components of the Communist Party-State ideology and actions are:

- *Marxist social evolutionism* is founded on a "natural" and "historical" hierarchy between societies with different steps of material, technical and political development (from feudal society and capitalist society to communist society)
- *Collectivisation of the means of production* is actions against the capitalist system to share resources and productions tools with equitable distribution for all.
- *Modernisation and industrialisation* used natural resources without limit as tools to achieve these goals of nation development to reach communist objectives.
- The main tools of this socio-economical and political system are a *very strong social, cultural and political control on the society*, because the final aim is to build the "New Socialist Man" for Revolutionary purposes to reach the "Perfect society".

---

[10] The presentation of Mrs Bui Linh Hue (Thai Nguyen University, Vietnam) about "A Ecocritical Study of the Discourses on Progress and Western Civilization by Early 20th Century Vietnamese Intellectuals", made at the ASLE Conference in Hanoi (2018), complete my demonstration of Vietnamese borrowings to French modernity.

4) Second Communist period (1986 until today)

The Second Communist period called « Transitional Period » begins with Đổi Mới Economical Reforms (1986) and continues today. The new national slogan is "Socialist-oriented market economy". In short, to achieve the ultimate communist goal one must use the capitalist system, as China did since the 1980s. From the analytical point of view, this is another aspect of Western naturalism mode of identification because according to Western capitalist ideology nature and non-humans don't have any rights, so they can be used to produce wealth and generate profits. On this point, Marxism and capitalism share the same relationship of uses of nature.

The main components of this transitional period are:

- *Marxist social evolutionism* needs to be adapted because the market economy will be a new support to build the socialist society.
- *The Private enterprises are often strongly connected with Party-State system.* These connections and the high level of corruption among officials allows a very low level of respect of the laws: This leaves a large open door for many offenses for the environment (massive deforestation, large-scale agricultural and industrial pollution).
- *The first national goal is economic development*, which is also a guarantee of political stability; for that, we rely on the use of natural resources. Economic development is the first, and the protection of the environment comes after, later.
- Even with important economic changes, we observe a strong cultural and political control on civil society and media (Internet, newspapers, social movements…);

Beyond the complexity of borrowing and syncretism processes (which we cannot detail here), the main thing to remember is how these ideas and practices will fit in superimposed layers. We observe this even if the new elements seem to contradict the old ones. As seems to be the case of Sino-Vietnamese traditional medicine based on analogies between natural substances and parts of the human body and technico-scientific medicine based on chemistry and modern physics. However, these elements are not mutually exclusive or not delete each other out. They are cohabiting. For example, it is usual for Vietnamese patients to follow a traditional medical treatment and at the same time a modern treatment. The fact that these treatments belong to two logical, two distinct modes of identification does not make any problem for the patient. In practice, in a pragmatic way, they can accumulate and syncretised by superpositions of more or less nested layers. However, detailed case studies of these ontological syncretisms are still missing for Vietnam.

We observe these different forms of syncretism both in discourses (see the very utilitarian dimensions of national development objectives) and the daily actions of Vietnamese (cults of sacred trees and forests on one side and the other side (serious industrial and domestic pollution...) in relation to nature today.

II - Examples of relations between nature and man in Vietnam, China and Japan

The three examples below of what "nature" means in Sino-Vietnamese world will make it possible to show the diversity of the means of expression of the relation to nature in the same mode of identification and at the same time the homogeneity of the type of exchange between human and non-human.

1) Learn to reach nature through practice

According to the Chinese philosopher Chuang Tzu (4th century BC): When men reach a very high level of mastery of their arts (religious rituals, studies of classical texts, technical and aesthetic through physical exercise or handicraft, etc.), they can act without mobilising their minds.

For example, an excellent wood-carver can take several decades to make his action on the wood without having to think about it. A kind of automatism both conscious and spontaneous made possible because man, material and action are no longer separated, or so little separated that they succeed in making totally One. The action is then done in a natural way, without effort and reaches its perfection. This action is then in conformity with Sky, which is natural and spontaneous (Billeter 2010). The action of man on the world is then in harmony with Sky and Earth, so by this way man can then reach nature. We find again the idea of governing in harmony with the cosmology which is at the center of the practice of management of men by traditional Chinese royalty. Man can access to nature by a long work on himself. So access to nature is achieved by a significant effort, a deep attention to non-human and actions and longtime training. This idea and practice are in opposition with the Western conception of nature where nature is thought of as something "given" that cannot be "acquired" by experience, conscience and training.

This first example also shows that ancient Chinese philosophical and ontological conceptions are often directly connected with very concrete or even technical practices, such as calligraphy, *Tai-chi-chuan*, wood carving, swimming in whirlpools or cutting of meat, etc. (Billeter, Levi). Thought and action are usually united in this world.

2) Integrate some powers of nature by eating them

China and Vietnam are two countries with a very high demand for wild meat from protected species for traditional medicine uses but also for cooking expensive dishes.

Thus the last rhinoceros was killed in Cat Tien national park (Southern Vietnam) in April 2010 for his horn that sold for 20.000 Euros. The last remaining tigers and bears are endangered because of the very high price for their meat. Chinese and Vietnamese believe that animal species are able to transmit/transfer their qualities to humans. By eating certain parts of these animals, humans can imbibe some of their physical and spiritual qualities. For example, meat and bones of tigers and bears are supposed to transmit the power of the animal, especially the sexual potency. The horn of Rhinoceros because it symbolically resembles a phallus are supposed to strengthen the sexual abilities of the man; it is the same for fresh snake blood. While the chemical composition of Rhinoceros horn is exactly the same as the human hairs and nails and snakes sexual abilities are rather mundane. These are symbolic actions and thought by analogy.

This is the same analogical thinking of the medical "doctrine of signatures[11]" in European Middle Age: "the leaves in the shape of eye look after the eyes"… This is an example, where human and non-human can share the same domain. Although different in their physicality and in their interiority, humans and non-humans can exchange physical abilities.

3) Building nature around the human

- Pagoda Gardens in Vietnam

For Vietnamese peasants of Red River Delta, we observed that for them nature is not a distant thing that one would encounter in the deep forests or in the mountains far from their own places of life, but nature is mainly around them, just next to them (Culas). In a milieu they know well and on which they act on a daily basis. According to them, nature is especially present in the gardens of pagodas, in their own gardens and in the big old trees at the crossroads (Przyluski, Stein, Dinh "Environnement, Homme"

---

[11] *Bennett (2007).*

and "Jardins au Vietnam"). This specific way of thinking and constructing nature contrasts sharply with the Western idea of "wilderness", protected from the attacks of human activities: A "virgin nature" thought out of any relation to man (Larerre).

- Satoyama: Biodiversity maintained by humans in Japan

The Japanese notion of *Satoyama* combines in a single word the idea of nature, of human and the relationship between them. *"Sato"* means "village and its agricultural lands" and *"Yama"* means "mountain and the maintained forests that make it up". Satoyama includes the environmental mosaic of forests, tree plantations, grasslands, farms, lakes and villages. This is a specific form of biodiversity maintained and built by humans. In 2010 at UNESCO assembly, Japan proposed to introduce the concept of Satoyama into international regulations on environment and biodiversity[12]. *Satoyama* means man and nature are not separated but necessarily connected by reciprocally influencing each other. The idea of "man made landscapes that build man" by Takeuchi is also central in A. Berque's demonstration (2014) to overcome and criticise Western dualism thought between human and nature.

To describe the relations woven between humans and non-humans in Satoyama, specialists speak of "socio-ecological landscapes" (Ichikawa). I think according to the examples above, it is possible to go further in the analysis of the meaning of "socio-ecological landscapes[13]". In a discrete but central way, the Satoyama diagram above presents the third perspective as "Recognition of the *value* and the importance of *local tradition* and *culture*" (my italics). But the content of this perspective is not only sociological and ecological; it asks to introduce other dimensions that are underlying in our examples above. The notion of "Value" is directly connected with ethics and religion, thus with the relationships between humans and non-humans, sometimes including immaterial beings (spirits and divinities, and all beings of the so-called "supernatural" world).

In fact, Satoyama is not only innovative because it integrates ecological and social dimensions and their reciprocal interactions, but it also opens the landscape to philosophical, ethical and religious dimensions.

---

[12] The Global Workshop on the Satoyama Initiative was held at UNESCO (Paris, 2010).

[13] See the history of invention of landscape in China (4th century) and Europe (16th century) (Berque 2013).

Conclusion

These three examples show the diversity of the conception of nature and non-human in the Sino-Vietnamese and Japanese world. In the first example, nature is the product of human learning after a long practice until the activity becomes an integral part of the human being. The second example shows how certain qualities of non-humans (animals or plants) can be integrated into the human body and mind-spirit. Finally, the last example shows how the idea of nature and biodiversity is not to be found in isolated, protected and supposedly "virgin" spaces, but rather in gardens and socio-ecological landscapes built and maintained by man. One of the common features of these examples seems to be that nature is not a self-defined and immutable state (as in the Western naturalism mode of identification), but this is the product of an action (examples 1 and 3) or the product of a relationship between human and non-human (examples 2). In the Western naturalistic mode of identification, nature is defined as a state of things, as an object. There is nature when there is no man. In the Sino-Vietnamese analogical mode of identification, nature is defined rather by types of actions and specific agreements between humans and non-humans. It is in a very particular relationship with humans that nature can be defined.

In the world, there is thus a wide variety of ways of how to conceive "nature" and the relationship between humans and nature. Many of them are still largely unknown. Often these relationships are only lived and acted by the local people, but there are not the object of philosophical and ontological discourses constructed. This is what we observed for Vietnam and for the populations of mountain ethnic groups in Vietnam, China, Laos and Thailand, but also for many forest populations in the Amazon or Siberia (Descola). In the case of China, some Taoist, Buddhist and Confucian schools of thought have for several centuries studied the relationship between man and nature, including political, medical, religious and metaphysical dimensions.

To describe, know and perhaps to understand the conceptions and practices of nature in different social groups of Vietnam (artisanal fishermen, collectors of plants and animals in the forest, rangers, mountain farmers, polluting industrialists ...) will allow to define what discourses on nature they are willing to hear and understand from a protection project, but also what they will be able to do in this direction. These different ways of speaking about nature and the possible protective actions will be built with local people and according to their conceptions and practices. But the protection project must still be able to integrate all the local dimensions of nature, so it must be able to challenge Western supremacy over the dual idea of Nature / Culture.

The analysis of human societies is usually based on three broad dimensions (economy, social and environment). But these three dimensions do not make it possible to describe for all the relationships that humans have with non-humans, and in particular with nature.

By introducing new dimensions, such as philosophical, ethical and religious, but also the emotional, affective and sensitive dimensions, because they produce meaning, channel or guide the relations between humans and non-humans, we will reach a more sophisticated level of understanding of the local realities. To characterise the new dimensions outlined above, often neglected in all kinds of studies, the Japanese geographer A. Berque (2013, 2014) speaks of "phenomenological" dimension, and the sinologists specialists in Taoism, J.-F. Billeter (2016) and J. Lévi (2003) speak of the "spontaneous" dimension.

Works Cited

Bass S., Annandale D., Phan, Van Binh, Tran, Phuong Dong, Hoang, Anh Nam, Le, Thi Kieu Oanh, Parsons M., Nguyen, Van Phuc, Vu, Van Trieu, eds. *Integrating Environment and Development in Viet Nam. Achievements, Challenges and Next Steps.* Hanoi: IIED, UNDP Poverty Environment Programme Vietnam, 2010. Print.

Batten, Bruce L., and Brown, Philip C., eds. *Environment and Society in the Japanese Islands: From Prehistory to the Present.* Corvallis: Oregon State University, 2015. Print.

Bennett, B. "Doctrine of Signatures: An Explanation of Medicinal Plant Discovery or Dissemination of Knowledge?" *Economic Botany* 61.3 (2007): 246-255. Print.

Berque, Augustin. *Thinking Through Landscape.* London: Routledge, 2013. Print.

---. *Poétique de la Terre.* Paris: Belin, 2014. Print.

Billeter, Jean-François. *Notes sur Tchouang-Tseu et la Philosophie.* Paris: Allia, 2010. Print.

---. *Études sur Tchouang-Tseu.* Paris: Allia, 2016. Print.

Bruun, Ole and Kalland, Arne, eds. *Asian Perceptions of Nature.* Copenhagen: Nordic Proceedings in Asian Studies No. 3. 1992. Print.

Cadière, Léopold. "Croyances et pratiques religieuses des Annamites dans les environs de Huê. I. Le culte des arbres. " *Bulletin de l'Ecole française d'Extrême-Orient* 18 (1918): 1-60. Print.

Culas, Christian. "Relations entre l'Histoire de la Gestion des Espaces Agricoles et l'Environnement au Vietnam". *Politiques environnementales en Asie du Sud Est.* Eds. Olivier Ferrari, Dominique Bourg. Paris: Karthala, (forthcoming), 2018. 275-324. Print.

---. "Study of Discourses on Local Knowledge and Practices on Environment Management in Vietnam Mountains." *Modernity and Dynamics of Tradition in Vietnam: Anthropological Approaches.* Eds. Luong Van Hy, Ngô, Van Le, Nguyen, Van Tiep, Phan, Thi Yen Tuyet. Ho Chi Minh City: Nha Xuat Ban Dai Hoc Quoc Thanh Pho Ho Chi Minh, 2018. 292-334. Print. (in Vietnamese).

Descola, Philippe. *Par-delà Nature et Culture.* Paris: Gallimard, 2005. Print.

Do, Thi Mai Hanh. "Transplanting Common Law Precedents: An Appropriate Solution for Defects of Legislation in Vietnam." *European Scientific Journal* 7.26 (2009): 48-70. Print.

Dournes, Jacques. "Le Monde Végétal du Montagnard Est-il Animé ? Observations en Pays Sre (Minorité Ethnique Montagnarde au Viêtnam). " *Journal d'Agriculture Tropicale et de Botanique Appliquée* I.5-6 (1954): 214-219. Print.

---. "Le Milieu Jörai. Eléments d'Ethno-Ecologie d'une Ethnie Indochinoise." *Études rurales* 53-56 (1974): 487-503. Print.

Dinh, Trong Hieu. "Environnement, Homme, Société. Impacts du Modèle 'Socialiste' au Vietnam." *Ho Chi Minh, l'Homme et son Héritage.* Eds. Marcel Bénichou and Bui-Xuan Quang. Paris: La Voie Nouvelle, 1990. 230-74. Print.

---. "Signes-Nature, Signatures, Biodiversité : les 'Bosquets Cultuels' au Vietnam. Pour un Concept de 'Vestiges Verts'." *Cahiers d'Etudes Vietnamiennes* 12 (1997): 31-44. Print

---. "Jardins au Vietnam : la Nature entre Représentations Culturelles et Pratiques Culturales." *Extrême-Orient, Extrême-Occident.* N° spécial "L'Art des Jardins dans les Pays Sinisés : Chine, Japon, Corée, Vietnam" 22 (2000): 135-51. Print. http://www.jstor.org/stable/42635702?seq=1#page_scan_tab_contents

---. "Sciences Sociales et Biodiversité: Articulations Entre le Global et le Local au Vietnam." *Revue Internationale des Sciences Sociales* 178 (2003): 639-643. Print. https://www.cairn.info/revue-internationale-des-sciences-sociales-2003-4-page-639.htm

Ichikawa, Kaoru. *Socio-Ecological Production Landscapes in Asia.* Nairobi: United Nations University Institute of Advanced Studies (UNU-IAS), 2012. Print.

Iwatsuki, Kunio. "Harmonious Co-Existence Between Nature and Mankind: An ideal Lifestyle for Sustainability Carried Out in the Traditional Japanese Spirit." *Humans and Nature* 19 (2008): 1-18. Print.

Latour, Bruno. *Politique de la Nature. Comment Faire Entrer les Sciences en Démocratie.* Paris: La Découverte, 2004. Print

Lee, Janghee. *Xunzi and Early Chinese Naturalism.* Suny Series in Chinese Philosophy and Culture. Albany: State Univ. of New York Press, 2005. Print.

Lévi, Jean. *Propos Intempestifs sur le Tchouang-Tseu.* Paris: Allia, 2003. Print.

Mus, Paul. *Planète Viêt-Nam. Petite Sociologie Visuelle.* Paris: Arma Artis, 1988. Print.

Nguyen Van Thang. "The Hmong and the Yao Peoples in Vietnam: Impact of Traditional Socioeconomic and Cultural Factors on the Protection and Development of Forest Resources." *The Challenges of Highland Development in Vietnam*. Eds. Rambo A. Terry, Reed R. Robert, Cuc Le trong and Di Gregorio M. R. Hawaii: East-West Center Program on Environment Honolulu, Hanoi Univ., Univ. of California, Berkeley, 1995. 101-119. Print.

O'Rourke, Dara. "Community-Driven Regulation: Towards an Improved Model of Environmental Regulation in Vietnam." *Livable Cities: The Politics of Urban Livelihood and Sustainability*. Ed. Peter B. Evans. Berkeley: Univ. of California, 2001. 95-131. Print.

O'Rourke, Dara. "Economics, Environment and Equity: Policy Integration During Development in Vietnam," *Berkeley Planning Journal* 10 (1995): 15-35. Print.

Ouyang, Yuzhi. *Les Caractéristiques de la Culture Traditionnelle Chinoise*. 2008. (unpublished paper)

Przyluski, Jean. "Note sur le Culte des Arbres au Tonkin." *Bulletin de l'Ecole française d'Extrême-Orient* 9.1 (1909): 757-764. Print.

Pham, Thi Thuong Vi and Rambo, Terry A. "Environmental Consciousness in Vietnam." *Southeast Asian Studies* (Japan) 41.1 (2003): 76-100. Print.

Sikor, Thomas O. and O'Rourke, Dara. "Economic and Environmental Dynamics of Reform in Vietnam." *Asian Survey* 36.6 (1996): 601-617. Print.

Stein, Rolf Alfred. "Jardins en Miniature d'Extrême-Orient." *Bulletin de l'Ecole française d'Extrême-Orient* 42 (1942): 1-104. Print.

Takeuchi, Kazuhiko. "Rebuilding the Relationship Between People and Nature: the Satoyama Initiative." *Ecological Research* 25 (2010): 891-97. Print.

Thomas, Frédéric. *La Forêt Mise à Nu : Essai Anthropologique sur la Construction d'un Objet Scientifique Tropical: "Forêts et Bois Coloniaux d'Indochine"*. Ph.D thesis History and Civilisation, Paris: EHESS, 2003. (unpublished paper).

USAID. *Vietnam Tropical Forest and Biodiversity Assessment*. Hanoi: US Foreign Assistance Act Report, 2013. Print.

Vu, Tan Phuong and Nguyen, Thuy My Linh. *Forest Ecological Stratification in Vietnam*, Hanoi: RCFEE, FAO, UN-REDD, 2011. Print.

Vuong, Xuan Tinh. "Customs of the Protection of the Forest and Resources in Integration with the Current Rules of the Villages at Tay and Nung." *Kien thuc ban dia cua dong bao vung cao trong nong nghiep va quan ly tai nguyen thien nhien*. Eds. Hoang Xuan Ty and Le Trong Cu. Hanoi: Nha Xuat Ban Nong Nghiep, 1998. 121-250. Print (in Vietnamese).

Zink, Eren. *Hot Science, High Water. Assembling Nature, Society and Environmental Policy in Contemporary Vietnam*. Copenhagen: NIAS Press, 2013. Print.

Websites

International Partnership for the Satoyama Initiative, n.d. (no date). Web. 15 June 2017. http://satoyama-initiative.org

Larrère, Catherine. "The Main Currents in Environmental Ethics" and "Scientific Models for the Protection of Nature." *Man and Nature- Making the Relationship Last. Biosphere Reserves.* Ed. L. Garnier, Paris, UNESCO, 2008. 26-31. Web. 16 December 2017. http://unesdoc.unesco.org/images/0015/001584/158417e.pdf

Lu, Shuyuan. *The Ecological Era and Classical Chinese Naturalism. A Case Study Tao Yuanming (365–427).* Springer online: China Academic Library Serie, 2017. Web. 12 December 2017.

Chapter 10

Tales from the Mouth of the River: Ecocritical Mythology and Philippine Epic Poetry

Timothy F. Ong,
University of the Philippines, Philippines

Abstract

The essay looks at how folk narratives interrogate the possibility of inquiring about the relationship of humans with the world through the mythology instantiated by folk poetics. It looks at the epic poem from Central Philippines entitled "Hinilawod" that is framed with and against nature. The essay ultimately provides a way to reimagine and reconstruct indigenous epistemologies in Philippine folk texts from an ecocritical/ecophilosophical lens through a riverine discourse in the poem

Key words: Hinilawod, ecophilosophical lens, indigenous epistemologies.

Folklore has always been considered to be a mirror of culture, as "autobiographical ethnography,"[1] that is, as people's own description of themselves. It is in folklore that a people's culture, materially manifested in rituals, poems, songs, or dances, that one is able to discern how folk consciousness made sense of itself and its relationship to the world. However, precisely in its autobiographical nature, folklore must never be taken as reality but rather as perception, one that might even be distorted in the name of self-imaging. Folklorist Vladimir Propp notes that in folklore, "[r]eality is not reflected directly but through the prism of

---

[1] Alan Dundes, *Meaning of Folklore*, ed. Simon J. Bronner (Logan: Utah State University Press, 2007), 55.

thought, and this thought is so unlike ours that it can be difficult to compare a folklore phenomenon with anything at all" because "[p]rimitive man sees the world of things not as we [in the contemporary] not as we do, and his views change from one to another."[2] Thus, reality can only be refracted through the "prism of thought," and this refraction is what constitutes what we now understand as folklore. This process of distortion becomes crucial in understanding folk consciousness primarily because even though it does not speak about an existential reality per se, it gives us instead an overview of the people's values and how they fashion themselves to be.

The value matrix and self-presentation instantiated by folklore are important when we talk about worldview, which is to say perspective. This paper is particularly interested in understanding a culture's perspective in folk literature, but a perspective that is focused not just on the people themselves but the people in relation to their world. In other words, it is an inquiry about the position, perception, and experience of humans with and within the natural world as articulated by the folk consciousness. How can this relationship be gleaned from folk literature, specifically in the Philippines, and what does this relationship say about the folk's conception of nature and the natural world at large?

It is in this light that I wish to propose a reading of the epic poem from Central Philippines entitled "Hinilawod" (Tales from the Mouth of the River) that is framed with and against nature. In short, how does one read the epic poem from an ecocritical point of view? How does one map out the interconnectedness of the human, by way of the epic hero, with nature and the natural? Finally, how does an inquiry about "nature" and the "natural" in the epic poem point to an articulation of an eco-conscious mythology? It is hoped that this paper provides a way to reimagine and reconstruct indigenous epistemologies in Philippine folk texts from an ecocritical/ecophilosophical lens.

Ecological Discourse in the Epic

Several similarities can be drawn from the different genres in folk literature, and one of these is an insight into the primordial experience of humans with the world at the moment of creation. As such, creation myths tell us how the world came to be and how its origins can be

---

[2] Vladimir Propp, *Theory and History of Folklore*, trans. Ariadna Martin, et. al., ed. Anatoly Liberman (Minneapolis: University of Minnesota Press, 1984), 10.

explained in a symbolic sense. If the myth is cosmogenic in nature, epics, on the other hand, are cosmologic and civilisational, that is, it is concerned about the ways in which humans are to reckon with their own humanity. Epics almost often include an inquiry about the implications of being human. For example, the epics caution us that even though "intelligence gives us a godlike potential to master our environment, we are limited by the deadly consequences of our not actually being gods," and that "human passions often interfere with intelligence,"[3] which could have dire consequences resulting from errors in judgment. At the root of this is really a question of mortality and the desire to outlive one's self. Thus, while myths explain the beginning of the world, epics instruct us how to live in it.

This pedagogical insight has several implications. First, epics foreground the relational aspect of humans not just with other humans, but with the non-human as well, that is, nature. This relationality is the premise of the ecological discourse in the epics: one does not just live in the world in solitude but is always already imbricated in a network of relationships. As such, the epics invite its readers to reimagine the wholeness of the cosmos as a product of relationships that bind this mythological world together. This network allows the contemporary reader to situate the human experience as imagined in mythic terms as contingent on its surroundings, which is to say that human consciousness is always determined by this ecology of relations that exists in the folk imagination rather than the other way around.

Second, the key feature of this relationality operates on the register of order such that to live within and in relation to the world is to tame its chaos, which ensures the civilisational logic embedded in epic poems, in order for the world to be populated. As the prime agent in the epics, the hero/ine seeks to understand the complex entanglements of this cosmos to be able to live within it. In the epics, the cosmos is understood to be full of peril such that it becomes the task of the hero/ine to make sense of the world by becoming familiar with the strange, and s/he does so by battling the threats that come his/her way. What is given importance in the epics is the ability of the human to establish this relationality but in a way that preserves its centrality in the order of things, which is to say that the ecological discourse here privileges the survival of the human by setting up the narrative of peril as one where the human must emerge victorious from the hazards caused by the yet-to-be-explored cosmos. Because of

---

[3] Katherine Callen King, *Ancient Epic* (West Sussex: John Wiley & Sons Ltd., 2009), 2.

this, human agency is imbued with the logic of discipline and control to subdue what is otherwise injurious to the survival of the human to ensure that the hero/ine continues the task of civilising the world. Therefore, what is chaotic is excised from the folk consciousness to reveal that the world can be understood as having a potential for order, which is the telos of the epic itself.

Lastly, this relationality is understood as anthropocentric primarily because it is through the exemplification of an idealised way of living that the epic makes its most convincing argument. It is through heroic deeds that people from a specific culture derive their lifeways because in struggling against the odds, the hero's struggle is "waged not for narrow, petty goals, not for personal interests, not for the well-being of the individual hero but for the people's highest ideals."[4] The epic hero, as emblematic of a people's culture, is placed in a conundrum at the start of the epic journey, and it is always the threat of one's own mortality. To counter this, the epic hero must be committed to triumph over struggles to achieve a goal, but "[i]n this full commitment to action he embodies the risk of death."[5] As such, the epic hero is always presented with the threat of annihilation that must be overcome to prove that indeed, s/he is exemplary in conduct and deeds. These antagonistic forces, which are driven by the death-instinct, place the epic hero in a very difficult situation that tests his/her character. This sense of risk, of impending mortality, charges the hero's journey with urgency and immediacy; otherwise, the epic poem loses its moralising feature of triumph over struggle.

In *Hinilawod*, we see that the premise of the epic journey is male degeneracy and possible impotency.[6] The epic starts with the retelling of the epic hero Humadapnon's dream, which sets the narrative in motion. As the activating instance of the epic, the epic hero is presented with the risk of self-effacement, which is a common motif in epic poems because of their capacity to establish a civilisational order to espouse a cultural identity.

---

[4] Propp, 149.

[5] Albert Cook, T*he Classic Line: A Study in Epic Poetry* (Bloomington: Indiana University Press, 1966), 3.

[6] F. Landa Jocano, *Epic of Central Panay 2: Hinilawod, Adventures of Humadapnon (Tarangban I)* (Quezon City: Punlad Research House, Inc., 2000), 9.

Gahumpaya sa duyan	He was in the hammock reclined
Gahantay sa ablongan	There he was idly lying down
Ibuasaw sa banwa	A young man of rightful age
Ilay-aw sa dinon-an	Yet a bachelor he remained
Nagaparibung domdom,	He was musing over his fate,
Nagapainu-inu.	Thinking of his future state.

Initially, the epic hero is in a state of stasis, which is how narratives often start, but he is perturbed by an external stimulus that gets internalised and eventually propels him to action. The problem here is clear: the epic hero is in the right age, but then the predicament is that his potency must be actualised by finding a wife that would not only provide him with offsprings to continue the process of establishing civilisational order as growth, but also one that should be his equal. This preoccupation with marriage has been noted by Jocano as a thematic concern that pervades the epic poem. Jocano notes in his analysis of *Labaw Donggon*, a shorter variation of the much longer *Hinilawod*, that the epic is concerned about marriage and, therefore, finding a wife is "the most desirable kind of existence in both the epic and contemporary life" such that the institution of marriage, understood as polygamous in the epic, was "necessary in order to have the world populated."[7]

The future state that Humadapnon ruminates, therefore, is one that reifies the organising principle inherent in civilisational discourse, but that which equally resists the continuity afforded by stasis. In short, in his dream, the epic hero confronts the most primal fear of humanity: the death of the self. He anticipates this death and must therefore overcome it by way of reproduction, but to triumph over that struggle requires him to find a suitable partner that has generative faculties in order to mark an imprint of the self onto the offspring. This relationality that is marked by the replication of the human by way of genealogical succession to populate the world is what constitutes the ecological discourse in the epic poem.

Nature and the Epic Hero

What, then, of nature? If the structure of the epic begins with the risk of sterility and must therefore end with marriage and consummation, what constitutes the middle? The gap is essentially the struggle that separates the epic hero from the desired outcome. The epic provides the instance where this anthropocentric notion of genealogical succession is threatened by way of the conflict, and in *Hinilawod*, the conflict is nature itself, that is, the sea.

"Magsalakay ka, Buyong, Magmamkaw ka sa tunga ka lawdon," Kuon tana'y Taghuy, Singhan 'i Duwindi. "Magliali kang lawdon May naman-an takon, Buyong, nga buntog Imaw to imong kaangay."	"Then go and travel, Buyong, Go and cross the surging seas," Slowly said Taghuy, Said Duwindi. "Go and dare the billowing sea For there afar I know, Buyong, of a lady fair Who can equal your noble birth."

The sea here is the figure that separates the epic hero's initial state of stasis and the epic triumph of marital bliss. The sea, therefore, becomes the trope of mystery and danger that makes the epic poem worthy of nominating a hero out of the struggles that he is yet to face because the hero is not so much concerned on "feeding the body, cultivating the land, and so on, or even on natural warfare; but rather on the ideal of facing the unknown unflinchingly."[8] Here, we see nature as the antagonistic force that prevents the anthropocentric notion of relationality to materialise, that is, the sea or nature itself, allows the human to confront its positionality in a network of relationships: the human begins to understand the self in relation to the non-self, and this otherness is precisely threatening and disastrous because it is not yet known. Thus, the sea is described in the epic poem as "bleeding" and "wild" with "a strong evil charm that would make men forget their home" and with "waves lashing their fury untold."[9] Thus, in *Hinilawod*, the conflict that demarcates the hero from his desire is the sea, which is to say precarity, unpredictability, mystery—all things that reside outside of the realm of logic and science.

Thus, what this implies is that in understanding the relationship of the human with nature in folk consciousness, what is not yet understood is forced to reveal its mystery so much so that it becomes legible because of the possibility of taming nature. Here, what is revealed to us is that the relationship of nature with the epic hero can be understood through

---

[7] F. Landa Jocano, *The Epic of Labaw Donggon* (Quezon City: University of the Philippines Press, 1965), 31—32.
[8] Cook, 17.
[9] Jocano, *Hinilawod*, 21—22.

dominance. The recourse provided by the epic to take control over the uncertainty of the sea is by means of technology: the boat.

The boat is that trope which allows for the epic hero to assert his dominance of the terra firma over the yonic sea. In carving out a similitude of terrestrial stability over the shaky surface of the billowing sea, the boat functions as a metonymy of control. It is then revealed that the epic hero has to rely on this technology because the epic hero and his brother Dumalapdap are unskilled in travel, especially in navigation, and must therefore skirt the littoral space of the shore, the cusp of certainty and mystery.[10]

"Buyong, duoya lang paagya Ada pasapgirana Isalakayang bulawan Indi mo palaktudon Nga iyag pabalantahon!"	"Buyong, just man your bark Along the shore. And never Let your golden boat depart Far from the shore or cross not Beyond the sight of land!"

The logic presented here is that the boat is "a floating piece of space, a place without a place, that exists by itself, that is closed in on itself and at the same time is given over to the infinity of the sea."[11] The boat, as magic technology, metonymizes this desire to pierce the expanse of the sea to find the maiden promised to Humadapnon in the dream, such that the travel itself becomes emblematic of this penetration towards the unknown if only to reveal the secrets that await on the other end of the shore. In this sense, the boat, as a moving piece of space that mimics the stability of the terrestrial stands in opposition with the sea that has to be feminized in relation to the masculine thrust of human exploration because the relationality presented here operates in the register of order, control, and dominion. However, what the epic presents is the liminal case presented by the littoral: that the hero must tread the sea carefully by just skirting the shore. Both land and water, then, as part of the natural world, presents "nature" with an ambivalent sexuality because it can be seen as metaphors for masculine control and feminine mystery, but it is also both and neither.

The ambivalence of nature becomes more palpable by the figure of Sinangkating Bulawan, who tried to seduce Humadapnon to enter her cave dwelling during the course of the epic journey. In her study of Luang

---

[10] Ibid., 20.

[11] Michel Foucault, "Of Other Spaces," *Diacritics* 16, no. 1 (1984): 27.

cosmology, Sandra Pannell notes of polymorphic figures, such as enchantresses, that present the alterity of nature itself. She notes that for the Luang people, this alterity is presented as "unregulated and ambivalent sexuality" where the human is constantly faced with the "dangerous ambiguity inherent in the constitution of their own human identity and that of other things."[12] As such, the relationship of the [male] epic hero and [ambivalent] nature is intimated by the presence of Sinangkati because her polymorphism is not entirely sexual but rather speciational. This ambivalence is caused by the blurring of the line between the human and the non-human because although both can have the same concerns, the latter's attributes and often aberrant behaviour "points to their transcendence of the human order, or perhaps to the extremes possibilities of the human condition."[13] This ambivalence becomes a central issue in trying to map out the ecological discourse in the epic primarily because of the possibilities of other kinds of identities that threaten the establishment of order and the imposition of dominion over nature. Thus, in the epic, when Humadapnon succumbs to the seduction of Sinangkati, it not only prevents the fulfillment of the epic quest but it also reveals his "animal-like nature [and] highlights the vulnerability of humans to [the enchantress'] bestial charms and unprovoked attempts at seduction."[14] Moreover, Pannell notes that figures such as Sinangkati "highlight the destructive and fatal consequences of uncontrolled reproductivity, expressed in [her] overly exuberant sexuality."[15] As such, genealogical succession must have an inherent logic of order and temperance for the relationship of the human with nature to remain anthropocentric. Otherwise, it would be considered "non-natural" because it betrays the logic of control.

Therefore, the epic hero, in his quest to tame nature, ultimately has to contend with the possibility of frustration, that the impediments to his journey function as a mirror to reveal that the futility of dominion because what is disavowed as "non-human," that is to say, beastly, wild, disorderly, which is nature itself, can be found in the deepest, most primal level of what it means to be human. This is the horror that the epic hero must

---

[12] Sandra Pannell, "Of gods and monsters: Indigenous sea cosmologies, promiscuous geographies and the depths of local sovereignty," in *A World of Water: Rain, Rivers and Seas in Southeast Asian Histories*, ed. Peter Boomgard (Leiden: KITLV Press, 2007), 85.

[13] Ibid., 87—88.

[14] Ibid., 83.

[15] Ibid., 86.

contend with: to find himself in the greater order of the natural world, one has to accept that the human is first and foremost a "natural" species, as existing and caused by nature, such that the binary between the human and nature is rendered, at the end, superfluous.

The Natural in Folk Consciousness

From the other end of the sea, the news of Humadapnon's capture inside the cave is made known to Nagmalitong Yawa, the daughter of Matanayon and Labaw Donggon, and who also happens to be the most powerful maiden *(binukot)* in the land, and, therefore, the maiden who will punctuate the erotic journey. Through the intercession of Humadapnon's spirit friends, Yawa hears about the unfortunate incident that has befallen the epic hero and comes to his aid.

And so the narrative begins and ends with Yawa, and we are led to suspect that it is through her character that the narratological trajectory of the epic finds fulfillment. As both the source and salve of the epic hero's capture, she gains insight into her role in the epic. She decides to rescue the epic hero not out of love, but rather because of honor and obligation. As ethnomusicologist Maria Christine Muyco notes on Jocano's version of the epic as chanted by Hugan-an, Yawa "does have a personal motive: being with Humadapnon completes her, and she, him."[16] Should she decide to abandon Humadapnon in the cave, she loses favor from the spirit guides and therefore her power as *binukot* faces the threat of enervation.

Because she is bound by honor to save Humadapnon, she decides to not make her absence known to her parents and thus proceeds to use her power as a *binukot* to change her corporeality. In this turn of events, she decides to create a substitute for herself from pillows and changes her real body into the likeness of a man. Therefore, she deploys a strategic maneuvering of gender reversal.

More than being the subject capable of transfiguration, Yawa is also the dazzling demon of Hiligaynon epic tradition, Yawa, from "yaua" (demonio[17], demon), which makes him/her otherworldly, both maleficent and magnanimous, a characteristic that adds yet another layer to the

---

[16] Christine Muyco, "Binukot to Nabukot: From Myth to Practice," *Humanities Diliman* 13, no. 2 (2016): 57.

[17] Diccionario de la lengua Bisaya—Hiligueyna y Haría de las islas de Panay y Sugbu, s.v. "yaua." From here on out, Diccionario will be used to refer to this work.

many turns that enable the figuration of his/her character. As this trickster-devil figure, Yawa is able to transform into Sunmasakay, who bears a very close resemblance to Humadapnon. This moment of transformation via the total inversion of the corporeality of the epic heroine does not imply a change of essence.[18] The epic notes of this recreation of the self ("Liwata 'i tubuan") to become a man, where "liwat" (from "liuan," otra vez,[19] again).

When the epic heroine attempts to rescue Humadapnon, she employs the same strategy of polymorphism by using her divine powers to transform her body into a male being. Should she refuse the rescue, she would lose favor from the spirits, and so being with Humadapnon completes Yawa, and the same is true for the epic hero. Here, the polymorphism is both sexual and speciational, and Yawa, at once man and woman, desired and desirer, the epic hero's "spirit double" becomes the figure that allows us to understand the symbiosis of the human and nature because "the destiny of each leads, inevitably, to the other."[20] Thus, human and nature in this sense become one, only because it is "human nature" to do so, which is to say, natural.

Thus, in the final scene of the epic, when Yawa (as Sunmasakay) was able to rescue Humadapnon, she refuses the reward that has been promised to the savior: the hand of the epic hero for marriage. In the end, this refusal is a move towards self-introspection on the part of epic hero concerning his relationship with the natural world at large. Humadapnon thinks he is to be married to Yawa, but Yawa retreats to the *binanugan* (where the hawk rests). She therefore replaces the hawk and communes with nature in her isolation. The marriage is reworked here from human to nature into nature to nature itself, by way of Yawa's insistence of solitude.[21]

---

[18] Sabrina Petra Ramet, Gender Reversals and Gender Cultures: Anthropological and Historical Perspectives (London: Routledge, 1996), 4. In "The Functions of Gender Reversals in Religious Mythology and Ritual," Ramet notes the ubiquity of gender reversals in sacred texts including the Aztec god Xolotl, an avatar of Quetzalcoatl, the Hindu Krishna, an avatar of the god Vishnu, the Olympian Greek Zeus, as well as in Mahayana Buddhism, and even in medieval Christianity.

[19] Diccionario, s.v. "liuan."

[20] Muyco, 57.

[21] Jocano, *Hinilawod*, 186.

Kambay sa tapaw-tapaw	Right on the very top
Ka batung binangunan	Of the stone *binangunan*
Masumpirang mapungko	Carefully crossing her legs
Magurang galupindang.	There she sat unconcerned.
[...] Hugiwan do palabut	[...] Since she did not want company
Wara don palangahid	She did not want to be disturbed
Tay Nagmalitong Yawa.	Nagmalitong Yawa.

In the epic's ending, what we see is a reworking of the ecological discourse that seems to preempt the narrative. By refusing the marriage, Yawa foregrounds a different kind of relationality that is not merely understood in the anthropocentric sense. Dominion over nature is not always the telos of human agency, such that a relationship with nature is fostered that is premised on a recognition that nature itself is also constituted by the many relationships it creates within itself, thereby displacing the human at the center of this network. By way of conclusion, this scene presents us the final moment of ecological discourse concerning the relationality of the human and nature: living with/alongside nature is natural, and so is living within it. To live within nature means that the relationality ceases to be anthropocentric, such that Humadapnon must now confront the failure of consummation and see that a relationality premised not just in terms of non-human reproduction can also be natural in the folk consciousness.

Works Cited

Cook, Albert. T*he Classic Line: A Study in Epic Poetry.* Bloomington: Indiana University Press, 1966.

Dundes, Alan. *Meaning of Folklore.* Edited by Simon J. Bronner. Logan: Utah State University Press, 2007.

Foucault, Michel. "Of Other Spaces." *Diacritics* 16, no. 1 (1984): 22—27.

Jocano, F. Landa. *Epic of Central Panay 2: Hinilawod, Adventures of Humadapnon (Tarangban I).* Quezon City: Punlad Research House, Inc., 2000.

—-. *The Epic of Labaw Donggon.* Quezon City: University of the Philippines Press, 1965.

King, Katherine Callen. *Ancient Epic.* West Sussex: John Wiley & Sons Ltd., 2009.

Méntrida, Alonso de. *Diccionario de la lengua Bisaya—Hiligueyna y Haría de las islas de Panayy Sugbu, y para las demás islas.* Manila, 1841.

Muyco, Christine. "Binukot to Nabukot: From Myth to Practice." *Humanities Diliman* 13, no. 2 (2016): 49—74.

Pannell, Sandra. "Of gods and monsters: Indigenous sea cosmologies, promiscuous geographies and the depths of local sovereignty." *A World of Water: Rain, Rivers and Seas in Southeast Asian Histories*, edited by Peter Boomgard. 71—102. Leiden: KITLV Press, 2007.

Propp, Vladimir. *Theory and History of Folklore*. Translated by Ariadna Martin, et. al. Edited by Anatoly Liberman. Minneapolis: University of Minnesota Press, 1984.

Ramet, Sabrina Petra. *Gender Reversals and Gender Cultures: Anthropological and Historical Perspectives*. London: Routledge, 1996.

Chapter 11

Animism in Southeast Asian Myths and Its Impacts on Acts of Environmental Protection

Nguyen Thi Mai Lien,
Ha Noi National University of Education, Vietnam

Abstract

The ancients believed that both living and non-living things had souls. Grass, flowers, birds, and other non-human animals also have souls. Natural phenomena were considered divine. Human beings and the universe had an intimate and magical connection. This idea is also seen in the myths of several other countries in the world. For example, in Japan, a religion worshiping the souls of all things (kami), called Shinto, exists to this day. The Southeast Asian region has similar beliefs, which influence the behaviour of local inhabitants towards nature and the environment. They live in harmony with nature and appreciate environmental protection instead of exploiting nature. My paper examines the ideas of animism in the myths of Southeast Asia and its impacts on environmental behaviours of ancient tribes in the region. The paper also addresses the question if animism is still alive today and how it can offer deep lessons for contemporary times with regards to environmental protection.

Keywords: Southeast Asian Animism, Environmental Protection.

Animism and its Presence in Ecocriticism

Animism is derived from the Latin word "anima" which means "breath, spirit, life". It is the belief that things and creatures have their own spirits. Animism is the oldest form of belief system in the world. Although each culture has different myths and rituals, "animism" is the most fundamental element in "spiritual" or "supernatural" concepts of native communities.

The most widely accepted definition of animism was one developed by Edward Burnett Tylor in the late nineteenth century. Tylor is the first academic who wrote about animism as one of the earliest notions in anthropology (Bird-David S67). In Edward Tylor's book *Primitive Culture* (1871), animism is seen as "the general doctrine of souls and other spiritual beings in general" (260). According to Tylor, animism includes "an idea of pervading life and will in nature" (260), which means a belief that all non-human natural objects have souls. This formulation was not different from what Auguste Comte calls "fetishism" (Adam 85). For Tylor, "animism represented the earliest form of religion, being situated within an evolutionary framework of religion which has developed in stages and which will ultimately lead to humanity rejecting religion altogether in favor of scientific rationality" (Graham 6). In 1869 (three years after Tylor proposed the definition of animism), John Ferguson McLellan argued that the belief that all things possess souls which were clearly expressed in fetishism gave rise to a religion that he called Totemism. He affirmed that the primitives had believed that they had inherited a number of traits similar to their totem (Adam 85).

Several ecocritics have recently attempted to understand the connections between animism and environmental consciousness of modern people and the impacts that animism has had on the modern conception of environmental protection. Greg Garrard asserts that although there is historical evidence about connections between animistic beliefs and a sustainable environment, these connections have not been theorized in detail within the fields of history, literature or ecology. The book explores relations of animistic traditions of the Native Indians in the United States with sustainable ecological practices in present-day contexts. While figuring out ways in which ecofeminism finds correlations between animism, ecology and feminism in Native Indian tribes, the book makes an argument that in the reading of modern ecocritical literature, it is necessary to believe that "devotional ecology" or animism is not only complementary to scientific ecology but has, in many instances, emerged as an aspect of environmental consciousness. Esthie Hugo in the article "Looking Forward, Looking Back: Animating Magic, Modernity and the African City - Future in Nnedi Okorafor's Lagoon (*Social Dynamics* 2017 43:1) analyses forms of existence in a world in which there is respect for (human) others, respect for plants, animals, inanimate things and invisible forces.

This paper affirms the fundamental importance of this attitude in that it breaks the familiar attention of Western intellectuals about the artificial division between one and the other, between man and the non-human world, or between people - the environment, culture and nature. This is a division that many Western cultures are trying to overcome in an effort to establish a more sensitive attitude towards the earth. Andy Fisher in *Radical Ecopsychology: Psychology in the Service of Life* (Albany: State University of New York Press, 2013) argues for the need of perceiving animism as a solution to an increasingly unproductive world, where people growingly feel alienated and separated from the universe. Animism is needed because it encourages people to feel connected to nature and has an emotional unconscious identity with natural phenomena. In this world there is no voice for stones, trees and animals, nor is there any human conversation with them that they can hear. Animism allows ecocritics to understand and describe human psychology as part of the natural world, a phenomenon of nature, including organisms and other entities.

Brendan Myer in the thesis *Animism, Spirit and Environmental Activism* (2000) affirms that animism is the metaphysical framework of knowledge in which human beings place all living things, realities, and themselves into it, because they do not assume a strict hierarchy of rank or dominance among living creatures. All these, the thesis argues, form a holistic environmental attitude. According to Myer, animism is a fundamental principle of environmental philosophy; it recognises a lasting relationship between man and the environment; it shows how all life, including human life, exists and remains within the boundaries of an integrated ecological system, that is, the world. It points to a way of thinking in the direction of the distinction between the environment and the human being that causes unnecessary suffering (towards both environment and humans) and environmental waste. Maheshvari Naidu's paper in A*nimated Environment "Animism" and the Environment Revisited* posits an analysis of the concept of animism and environmental correspondence and simultaneously predicts the possibility of the harmony of animism and "spiritual tendencies" in contemporary environmental consciousness. In "Relational Epistemology, Immediacy, and Conservation: Or, What Do the Nayaka Try to Conserve?" (*Journal for the Study of Religion, Nature and Culture*, 2, 1, 2008, 55-73) and "Animism" Revisited: Personhood, Environment, and Relational Epistemology (*Current Anthropology, Vol. 40, No. S1, Special Issue Culture—A Second Chance?* (February 1999), pp. S67-S91), Nurit Bird-David affirms that spiritual practices form a specific cultural and indigenous understanding. Bird-David criticises the view that animism is a simple religion and a failed knowledge and offers ways in which animistic ideas work in the sphere of social practice and particularly in the constructs of locality between man and the relation of concepts of environmental ecology. In complementing ecocritical interpretations of animism and modern thinking of the environment, this paper examines the existence of animism in Southeast Asian myths and its impacts on constructions of relationships between humans and nature in the region. Studying animism in myths of some Southeast Asian countries in relation to modern scholarship about the environment, this paper emphasises the attitudes of respect and worship that the native people in Southeast Asia have towards nature. The study of myths reveals that the ancients must have shown their caring attitude, respect, and protection towards natural habitats. This paper argues that studying animism in myths is a form of ecocriticism.

Animism in Southeast Asian mythology

Like myths of other nations in the world, the Southeast Asian myths were born in primitive times when humans were dependent on nature for survival. People were explaining natural phenomena with their imagination and a sense of the homologous self. As such, natural phenomena were associated with spiritual aspects. Specifically, Khmer groups in Cambodia believe in God Soil, God Water, God Fire, God Wind, and God Fauna (Chouléan). Meanwhile, the Laotian people called the spirit of animals and plants, and natural phenomena *thẻn* (god) and *phi* (ghost). *Thẻn* is the deification of natural phenomena, and *phi* is the sacrification of animals and plants. *Thẻn* and *phi* have their own place in the heavens, not in the same section with humans. *Thẻn* and *phi* divide the world into separate sections for governance. Governing the upper part of the world is *thẻn Luông* (God of Heaven), and the underworld is governed by thẻn Water, thẻn Sun, thẻn Rain, and thẻn Wind. *Phi* is also divided into many forms to manage different parts of the earth: house's ghost, commune's god, forest's ghost, river's ghost. In old Laotian belief, the image of *thẻn* and *phi* are used to explain the origins of the universe and natural phenomena. For example, in the myths *Giving birth to soil and water, Bua La Phan,* and *The Creation of the World, thẻn* Sky created the heaven, the earth, mountains, rivers, and modelled the moon, the sun, stars and humans from the chaos by his own breath, hands and strength.

In Burma, the Burmese also express their faith in spirits of all things through myths of natural phenomena and animals and plants. They call their spirits *nats*: *nat* Soil, *nat* River, *nat* Mountain, *nat* Tree, *nat* Rice, etc. They believe that the universe, humans, nations, ethnic groups, ancestries, and lords are all derived from and blessed by *nats* to be survived and developed. A common myth explaining the human origin in Myanmar emphasises that people's survival is blessed by spirits of trees: Once upon a time when there were no humans on earth, and nine Biamma gods left the heaven and came down to earth. First, they begged the Sun, the Moon, and Stars for light. The Sun, the Moon, and Stars were moved by the entreaties, and they gave the gods light. Tasty soil was their first food. They ate until such food ran out, and then they ate *paxalata*, a kind of liana to survive. Then paxalatas were gone, they looked for thalesan tree, a flavoured rice, to eat to make their bodies stronger. (*Luu Duc Trung 178; Obayashi 43-66; Scott 118*). The Burmese believe that it is the gods that govern natural phenomena that bring humans the source of light and food. Moreover, Burmese legends also demonstrate a common belief in the existence of spirits in natural resources: A dragon princess living in the mountain to the north of Myanmar copulated with God Sun and gave birth to three dragon eggs. Consequently, God Sun was very happy, immediately sent her a ruby to build kingdoms for their children. Unfortunately, on the way from heaven to the earth, a merchant fraudulently replaced ruby with buffalo dung. The princess received the dung, getting so distressed and frustrated that she had a stroke and died. Three dragon eggs were dropped into a river. One egg hit a reef, bursting to countless rubies. Another egg fell to the central region of Myanmar and transformed into a tiger. The last fell to the south and transformed to a crocodile" (Luu Duc Trung 181; Morgan 15-16; U Khin Maung Nyunt 269-289). The story explains in an animistic way that all plants and animals in Myanmar are gods by their origin.

In myths of Indonesia, the origin of the world and its natural phenomena are seen as the products of gods' creation. As told, at first, the world was a messy mix of light, foam, and steam. Then, a god created the first three components: earth, water, and heaven which then formed the main materials of the earth. The god's children who lived on the earth cramped living in a tiny space; they returned to heaven. The first child became Thunder god; the second became Lightning god; the third Rain god; the fourth Flood god; the fifth Thunderstorm god; the sixth Earthquake god; and seventh Rainbow god. The myth indicates a strong deification of the natural world in Indonesia (Dupré 80-85). Similarly, in traditional Thai folk culture, some sacred spirits play important roles in agriculture and associated natural phenomenon. For example, *Phosop* is the traditional and ancient rice goddess, whom Thailand people believe that to be blessed by her they must perform a periodic ritual called *Cha Laeo*. In Thailand, female entities that reside in trees are known as *Nang Mai, Lady of the Tree* or *Lady of the Wood*. *Nang Tani* is a female spirit who resides in banana trees and is usually present on full moon nights. For Thai people, souls or ghosts are elsewhere: in trees, in houses, in mountains and in forests. (Nguyen Duc Ninh 133; MacPherson 10-30; Guelden 208)

In Vietnam, the belief that all natural objects have their own souls is also very popular. The ritual of worshipping *Tứ phủ* [four palaces] of the goddesses of clouds, rain, thunder and lightning, is indicative of such belief. This ritual is practiced largely in provinces in northern Vietnam such as Ha Noi, Bac Ninh, and Ha Nam. When Buddhism migrated to Vietnam, the practice of worshiping the four gods was honoured with Buddha in temples.

Besides worshipping natural phenomena, the ancient Vietnamese people also worship geographical areas, which is evident in *Đạo Mẫu* [the worship of mother goddesses in Vietnam]. Đạo Mẫu worships four goddesses that represent four main geographical areas of the earth: *Thiên phủ* [Heaven Palace], the superior palace, governs the heaven, managing rain, storm, thunder and lightning. Nhạc phủ [Forest Palace], the second palace, takes care of the forest and provides food for beings. Thủy phủ [Water Palace] the third palace, reigns over rivers, facilitating wet rice and fisheries. Địa phủ [Soil Palace), the forth palace, controls the land, the source of all life (Ngô Đức Thịnh). The ritual of worshipping four goddess palaces demonstrates a popular animistic belief in Vietnamese culture.

Moreover, myths in Vietnam also indicate the presence of animism. For example, the sun appears in Vietnamese myths as a spirit dwelling on a carriage carried by humans. In winter, the sun is carried by strong young men so it can move very fast from the east to west. This story is to explain in a mythic way the natural phenomenon that daytime in winter is for a short duration. In summer, gods are carried by weak old seniors, so daytime in summer is much longer. Meanwhile, the god of the sea is imagined to be a giant turtle lying on the ocean floor. When the god breaths in, the ocean water descends, which aims to explain tidal phenomena. Moreover, the myth of *Son Tinh – Thuy Tinh* [The Genie of the Mountains and the Genie of the Waters] explains the phenomenon of annual floods at river deltas in northern Vietnam and the achievements of dealing with the flood in ancient Vietnam. Specifically, Son Tinh is the divine form of the phenomenon of annual floods in the Red River Delta, which destroy crops and lives of the local residents. Images of Thuy Tinh lifting the mountain up against the flood is reminiscent of the image of the ancient Vietnamese building dikes and damping up to protect themselves from the floods (Huu Ngoc 315; Nguyen Thi Thanh Binh and Healy 146-148).

It is also in Vietnamese belief that long-living animal species can transform into goblins that turn into a support-system for people or be a bad influence on people. The legend of *Lac Long Quan* and *Au Co*, widely-believed to be ancestors of the Vietnamese, tells the story of fairy father

Lac Long Quan defeating fish goblin, fox goblin, and tree goblin. The fish is described as follows: it lives for a long time; its body is fifty stick at length; its tail is like a sail; its mouth can swallow ten people at a time. When it swims, waves soar, boats sank, and all people on board were swallowed up. Fishermen are very afraid of that monster, calling it fish goblin (Fjelstad and Nguyen Thi Hien 22-23; Vo 20). Images of fox-goblin in the Vietnamese myths is of a nine-tailed fox that can live for more than a thousand years. It resides in a deep cave, at the foot of a rocky mountain. This goblin often transforms into a human figure, infiltrating itself into the people and abducting girls to the cave (Kröger and Anderson 80). Not only animals, flora is also believed to able to transform into goblins: it is commonly told that in Phong Chau, an area nearby Red River Delta, there was once an old tree called Sukaramaddava, thousands of feet in length, and its lush foliage was covered with a vast landmass; many years later, the tree withered and turned into a goblin which is usually called tree-goblin. This goblin was very devilish and extraordinarily insidious; it did not have a certain residence, it appears everywhere, transforms into different figures, for the purpose of capturing animals and humans for food (Bùi Văn Nguyên 185)

Belief in the spiritual nature of all things is a pervasive and lasting cultural belief in Southeast Asian communities. Although each ethnic group in the region has their own myths and possesses different explanations about the origins of the universe and the geographical and natural phenomena, they express a shared perspective that all things have souls and deserve respect. This paper shows how this shared belief has impacted environmental awareness of the Southeast Asians and if this belief remains and influences on the acts of environmental protection of peoples in modern time.

Impacts of Animism on Acts of Environmental Protection

It is possible to say that animism played an important role in the environmental consciousness of Southeast Asian people in the past as well as in the present. Believing that all things had souls, Asian natives did not only deny destructive acts towards the environment but also worshipped them. The ancient Vietnamese built shrines in villages, worshipping banyan trees in order to protect the trees as well as to be protected by the gods of the banyan trees. Consequently, trees of thousands of years old are protected, not being cut down. Many Vietnamese villages even considered the ancient trees as the guardians of the villages, such as the banyan tree, the goddess of Tien village, Kim Thai commune, Vu Ban district (Nam Dinh). In the present-day context, the villagers still share stories about the sacredness of this tree with each other. It is said that during wartime no guerrillas were arrested by enemies when they hid under the tree. There has never been a fatal accident in the 200m radius of the tree. Therefore, the villagers, from time immemorial construct the shrine to worship this ancient tree so that the tree spirit continues protecting the villagers from harm.

The custom of worshipping fish, such as the Whale Worshipping in coastal fishing villages of central Vietnam, still exists today. Fishermen believe that the whale is a guardian spirit that is sacred and friendly; it presents itself only for the purpose of supporting people. If fishermen have an accident at sea while fishing, the whale spirit will appear to save them. Therefore, whales are usually called ông [grandfather or sir] and protecting whales becomes an ethic of the local fishermen. When whales die, fishermen and other villagers hold a solemn funeral and build shrines to worship them.

Moreover, many ethnic groups in Vietnam practice rituals of worshipping gods of natural objects such as God of the Forest, God of the Mountain, and God of the Stream, showing them their gratitude and respect for their being protectors. These rituals form the culture of forest protection in many ethnic communities in Vietnam. For example, the feast of forest god of the ethnic group Pu Péo in Ha Giang, a mountainous northern province of Vietnam, has long existed through many generations of Pu Péo people. The festival is held on the sixth day of the sixth month in the lunar year, the time when the Pu Péo ethnic people think is the brightest and purest; thus heaven and earth are more sacred. The offering ceremony is prepared diligently. Each family prepares goats, chickens, rice, and wine as their offerings. This ritual demonstrates a beautiful culture in Pu Péo people that is the culture of protecting the forest. Liu Linzan, a researcher of cultures in Ha Giang province, states that

> [t]he worship of the forest gods aims at supporting the villagers' health, bringing good food, prosperity, and lush crops [...]. In the village where Pu Péo people live, the forest is always preserved.
> (*Lễ cúng thờ rừng*).

Besides being a spiritual ritual, the ceremony of worshipping the Forest god bears a real meaning, that is, it constantly reminds people to protect the forest as well as to preserve natural beauties of Ha Giang's rocky mountain areas (Lê Đại Duy 249-260; Trần Văn Ái).

Like Pù Péo in Ha Giang, Katu ethnic people in the Central Highland region of Vietnam also have their own perception and practice of animism.

In their culture of choosing land to establish villages, the Katu highlight the belief that places where there are forests, rivers and streams are places where it is possible to build new villages that can exist and are thus conducive for a family life. For Cowtu people, the forest is not just a living ecosystem of plants, animals and grass, but also a source of culture because they believe that forests are the guardian gods that protect them from cannibal animals and other enemies. Therefore, Katu always consider the forest as the Great Spirit, the great benefactor of the village. They also believe that if deforestation takes place, forests will punish human beings by making them sick, not giving them the capacity for giving birth to children; thus, the whole village will be infected and disaster will strike. Therefore, one village of the Katu named Kiet has set up many customary laws to make sure that no one would harm the forest. For example, there is the law strictly regulating shifting cultivation and cutting trees for housing (Phan Đăng Nhật *Đại cương* 130-150; Phan Đăng Nhật *Văn hóa các dân tộc tập 2* 120-123). Cơ Lâu Nhấp, the oldest headman of Lăng commune, said:

"Works of slash and burn cultivation are discussed carefully by village seniors and elders. Families are accepted to swidden fields only when they meet requirements related to the use of land and forest that are decided by the village patriarchs" (*Độc đáo*). He explained in detail that the requirements include not forest land cultivated are not so young, not old; an absolute ban on cultivating grave land and sacred forests - forests with many precious kinds of wood- and watershed forests. In order to emphasise the rigor in the regulation of forest protection of Lăng community, he said that headmen and seniors of the village usually hold meetings to give decisions on which trees to be cut down and where to make the cutting on the selected trees so that not to harm the seedlings, sacred forests of their village and villages of others.

Since time immemorial, the Katu in Tây Giang district (Quang Nam province) are always aware of their responsibility to protect the forest. They imparted to the descendants the love of forests, the sense of cherishing and worship tree gods and forest gods, so that they do not invade and exploit rare old forests illegally. Therefore, although the Katu live mainly on slash-and-burn cultivation, they still retain the precious woods such as lima, pomelo, cherry, and thousand-year-old banyan trees. The forest covers 70% of the natural area of the district. The most famous are forests of rare woods such as *erythrophleum fordii* forests (in Lăng commune), and the two-thousand bois de Siam tree garden (in Tr'hy and Aan communes), of which 725 are Vietnamese heritage trees. It is apparent that it is the worship of forest gods that make Tây Giang district a beautiful, green forest-covered area. This means the climate in the Tây Giang is very cool, to the point that it is told to be like "a refrigerator hanging in the sky." Tay Giang has become an ecotourism area attracting many visitors (*Góp phần tìm hiểu*).

Not only Pu Péo and Katu, the Mong ethnic people in Lai Châu and Lào Cai provinces also have the custom of worshiping forest gods. The forest worshipping festival of the Mong people in Tung Qua Lin commune, Phong Tho district, Lai Chau province is held on the day of the Dragon day of the first lunar month every year to pray for good weather, good harvests, and green forest. Forest worship demonstrates a deep message to people that they should always love forests, never cut down forests or cause fires to forests for slash-and-burn cultivation. The divine forest will bless mankind's peaceful life. As the consequence of such an animistic belief, Tung Qua Lin maintains more than 3,000 hectares of forest, including many primary forests, with many large trees that even cannot be held by two people's arms (Nguyễn Tuấn Hào; Rapin).

Southeast Asians live mainly on rice as their staple food. So far, in the region, rice paddy is considered a divine god. In Java, the rice god is imagined as a goddess called Dewi Sri. Javanese believe that men are not allowed to be near the goddess; thus they are not prohibited from many works in the process of growing rice such as sowing seeds, plowing, and cultivating rice. At harvest time, after the rice is transferred to the store, people held a marriage ceremony for the goddess and the male god Wisna with the purpose of praying for the season to bumper (Pigeaud 328; Meer 102-110; Sharma 45). In Malaysia, rice is called Princess Semangat Padi. Malays hold many rituals to ensure rice trees to be well planted and harvested. Malaysians absolutely forbid anyone to knock on the grain for the fear that Princess Rice would scare away. In some regions, Malay people consider rice as a beautiful, fragile princess that needs to be pampered and loved. They call her Sun Princess or Crystal Princess. At the beginning of the sowing season, or in the harvest season, they do rituals of cherishing a handful of grains so that they are not harmed by devils. The first rows of rice will be cut with small sickles to avoid making the rice plant unhappy. People choose the best seven rows of rice, carefully store them for the next season. That is the way they invite the rice soul home ("Malaysia: The Rice Soul- Myths"; Sharma 45; Nguyen Duc Ninh 200).

For the Thai people in Thailand, they hold the rice ritual when rice paddy starts growing. The ceremony is very formal with many gifts of fruits such as banana and cane. Since rice is seen as a goddess, people also offer her chalks, perfumes and combs. They sprinkle perfume on her body and brush her hair in the hope of making the goddess happy, so that the goddess will flourish and consequently the harvest will thrive (Young 140-145).

In Vietnam, different ethnic groups have specific rituals of worshipping rice trees. The Khmer called rice Mother. Rice Mother is imagined as a woman riding a fish, her hands holding rice. Meanwhile, Khmú ethnic group imagines rice as a white girl in the upland fields. For Bahnar, rice is Yangsri; this goddess decides life fate of human beings. Thus, the Bahnar hold many rituals expressing their thankfulness for rice, such as the feast of Sanok to show their respect for new rice seeds. The Cotu ethnic group in the Central Highland region traditionally worships Grandparents Rice. They occupy the best place in the kitchen to worship Grandparents Rice. On the altar of the rice god is a tơru, a bamboo-woven basket hung on the kitchen stool, in which there are beautiful clothes and small boxes of rice. People choose the best new grains to put in those boxes. When people change places of residence, they will also carry and will continue to worship the tơru in their new resident place. When the rice is harvested, people block all the ways to the fields by hanging the branches so that no strangers can enter. When they finish the rice harvest, they celebrate the new rice with a sacred festival: every house cooks new rice, put cooked rice into the basket and bring to share with each other. The more people give, the happier their ancestors are and the more blessings they will have. Meanwhile, young people dance to welcome new seasons.

Thus, animism has survived to this day and is richly represented in many forms in many cultures in Southeast Asia. Animism has a strong influence on the way of dealing with the nature of Southeast Asian people from ancient to present. They worship nature, living in harmony with nature; they do not invade and destroy nature. It is apparent that animism is a spiritual resource of Southeast Asia because it provides spiritual bases for people to criticise ideas and practice that tend to dominate nature and create environmental destruction. Moreover, animism helps to construct in cultures of the region a shared sense of environmental protection. With such argument, this paper complements existing ecocritical scholarship about animism and modern environmentalism that has developed by scholars such as Bird David, Garrad, Fisher and many others while also suggesting the need of further comprehensive research on role of animism in answering problems in dealing with environment and exploiting natural resources in present-day in Southeast Asian countries.

Works Cited

Bird-David, Nurit. "Animism" Revisited: Personhood, Environment, and Relational Epistemology." *Current Anthropology*. Vol. 40, No. S1, 1999, pp. S67-S69.

Myers, Brendan. *Animism, Spirit and Environmental Activism* (dissertation). Ottawa: National Library of Canada, 2001

Bùi, Văn Nguyên. *Việt Nam: Thần thoại và truyền thuyết*. Hanoi: NXB Khoa học Xã hội, 1993.

Chouléan, Ang. "The Place of Animism within Popular Buddhism in Cambodia: The Example of the Monastery." *Asian Folklore Studies*, Vol. 47, No. 1, 1988, pp. 35-41.

Dupré, Wilhelm. *Religion in Primitive Cultures: A Study in Ethnophilosophy*. The Hague: Mouton, cop. 1975.

"Độc đáo "văn hóa kiêng cữ, giữ rừng" của người Cơ tu ở Tây Giang." *Công an thành phố Đà Nẵng*, 18 May 2018, http://cadn.com.vn/news/71_189635_doc-dao-le-hoi-cung-than-rung-cua-nguoi-co-tu.aspx. Accessed 1 June 2018.

Đức Ninh (chủ biên). Văn học Đông Nam Á. Hanoi: NXB Đại học Quốc gia, 1999.

Fisher, Andy. *Radical Ecopsychology: Psychology in the Service of life*. Albany: State University of New York Press, 2013.

Fjelstad, Karen; Nguyen Thi Hien. *Possessed by the Spirits: Mediumship in Contemporary Vietnamese Communities*. Ithaca: Cornell University, Southeast Asia Program Publications, 2018.

Hugo, Esthie. "Looking Forward, Looking Back: Animating Magic, Modernity and the African City - Future in Nnedi Okorafor's Lagoon." *Social Dynamics* Vol 43, No.1, 2007, pp. 46-58.

Huu Ngoc. *Sketches for a Portrait of Vietnamese Culture*. Hanoi: The Gioi Publishing House, 1995.

Góp phần tìm hiểu văn hóa Cơ-tu. Hanoi: Social Sciences Publishing House, 2006.

Guelden, Marlane. *Thailand into the Spirit World*. Singapore: Times Editions, 1995.

Jaruworn, Poramin. "The *Roles* of the *Buddha in Thai Myths: Reflections* on the *Attempt* to *Integrate Buddhism into Thai Local Beliefs*" *MANUSYA: Journal of Humanities*, No.9, No.?, 2005, pp. 15-26.

Kuper, Adam. *Reinvention of Primitive Society: Transformations of a Myth* (2nd Edition). Florence, KY, USA: Routledge, 2005.

Lê, Đại Duy, Đức Thanh Triệu. *Các dân tộc ở Hà Giang*. Hanoi: The Gioi Publishing House , 2004.

"Lễ cúng thần Rừng và phong tục giữ rừng của dân tộc Pu Péo," *Hà Giang online*, 11 July 2008, http://www.baohagiang.vn/van-hoa/tin-tuc/200807/le-hoi-cung-than-rung-cua-dan-toc-pu-peo-504365/. Accessed 20 July 2018 .

Lưu, Đức Trung. *Văn học Đông Nam Á*. Hanoi: NXB Giáo dục, 1999.

Macpherson, Darcy. *Tree Spirituality: An Introduction to Trees, Humans, and the Realm They Share*. Bookbaby 2015, 1998.

Maheshvari Naidu. "ANimated Environment "Animism" and the Environment Revisited", *Journal of Dharma*, Vol. 36, No. 3, 2011, pp: 257-273.

"MALAYSIA: The Rice Soul- Myths, History and Folklore of RICE Beras or Nasi." *Earthstoriez*. 13 Ocb.2014. https://www.earthstoriez.com/malaysia-myths-history-folklore-rice/. Accessed Nov 26, 2018.

Meer, N. C. Van Setten van der. *Sawah cultivation in ancient Java, aspects of development during the Indo-Javanese period, 5th to 15th century*. Canberra: Faculty of Asian Studies, Australian National University, 1986.

Morgan, Diane. *Fire and blood: rubies in myth, magic, and history*. Westport, Conn.: Praeger, 2008.

Myers, Brendan. *Animism, Spirit and Environmental Activism* (dissertation). Ottawa: National Library of Canada, 2001

Nguyễn, Thị Thanh Bình, Dana Healy. *Aspects of Vietnamese Culture: Reading Materials for Advanced Students of Vietnamese Studies*. Hanoi: The Gioi Publishing House, 2002.

Nurit Bird David, "Animism" Revisited: Personhood, Environment, and Relational Epistemology." *Current Anthropology*, Vol. 40, No. S1, 1999, pp. S67-S91.

Kröger, Lisa; Melanie Anderson . *The Ghostly and the Ghosted in Literature and Film: Spectral Identities*. Newark: University of Delaware Press, 2015.

Ngô, Đức Thịnh. *Đạo Mẫu ở Việ ̂t Nam*. Hanoi: Va ̌n hóa - tho ̂ng tin, 1996.

Phan, Đăng Nhật. *Đại cương về văn hóa dân tộc thiểu số ở Việt Nam*. Hanoi: NXB Thời đại, 2012.

Nguyễn, Tuấn Hào and others. "Benefits of Phaseolus calcaratus in upland farming in northern Vietnam." *Voices From The Forest Integrating Indigenous Knowledge into Sustainable Upland Farming*. Ed. Malcolm Cairns. Washington, DC: Resources for the Future, 2007.

Obayashi, Taryo. "Anthropogenic Myths of the Wa in Northern Indo-China." *Hitotsubashi Journal of Social Studies*, Vol.3, No. 1, 1966, pp. 43-66.

Phan, Đăng Nhật. *Va ̂n hóa da ̂n gian các da ̂n to ̣c thie ̌u so ̌: nhũng giá trị đa ̣c sa ̌c*. Hanoi: NXB Đại học Quo ̌c gia Hà No ̣i, 2011.

Pigeaud, Theodore G.Th. *Java in the 14th Century: A Study in Cultural History*. Dordrecht: Springer, 1963.

Rapin, Ami-Jacques, Huy Khue Dao, Huy Tien Pham. *Ethnic Minorities, Drug Use & Harm in the Highlands of Northern Vietnam: A Contextual Analysis of the Situation in Six Communes from Son La, Lai Chau, and Lao Cai*. Hanoi: The The Giioi Publishing House, 2003.

Scott, James George. *Burma: a Handbook of Practical Information*. [Place of publication not identified] : Nabu Press, 2010.

Sharma, Shatanjiw Das. *Rice: Origin, Antiquity and History*. Boca Raton: FL CRC Press, c 2010.

Tylor, Edward Burnett, *Primitive Culture: Researches into the Development of Mythology, Philosophy, Religion, Art, and Custom.* Cambridge: Cambridge University Press, 2010.

Trần, Văn Ái. *Văn hóa dân gian của dân tộc Pu Péo ở Việt Nam.* Hanoi: NXB Văn hóa - Thông tin, 2011.

U Khin Maung Nyunt. "Reintegrating Into the International Community: Opportunities and Challenges for Myanmar" Sein, Chaw Chaw, Chenyang Li Xianghui Zhu. *Myanmar: Reintegrating into the International Community.* Singapore: World Scientific Publishing Co. Pte. Ltd 2016: 269-289.

Vo, Nghia M. *Legends of Vietnam: An Analysis and Retelling of 88 Tales.* Jefferson: McFarland & Company Inc., 2012.

Young, John E. De. *Village Life in Modern Thailand.* Berkeley, Calif.: University of California, 1958.

Bionotes of Contributors

Chi Pham (Ph.D.) is a tenure-researcher at the Institute of Literature in the Vietnam Academy of Social Sciences. She completed her Ph.D. in Comparative Literature at the University of California, Riverside (USA). Her dissertation, her researcher articles and conference presentations delve examine Vietnamese literature and politics. Of late, Chi has become increasingly interested in the field of literature and environment; she was the Chair of the organising committee of the second ASLE-ASEAN conference in Hanoi (January 2018), for which she put together the call for paper. Chi's native knowledge of Vietnamese culture and literature will add a dimension of authenticity.

Chitra Sankaran (Ph.D.) is an Associate Professor in the Department of English Language and Literature, NUS. Her research interests include South and Southeast Asian fiction, feminist theory and ecocriticism. In 2012 she published with SUNY Press, *History, Narrative and Testimony in Amitav Ghosh's Fiction.* Her other publications include monographs, edited volumes on Asian Literatures, chapters in books and research articles in IRJs including Journal of Commonwealth Literature, ARIEL, Theatre Research International, Journal of South Asian Literature, Australian Feminist Studies and Critical Asian Studies. She is an invited contributor to the Oxford History of the Novel in English (OHNE) series. She is currently working on ecofeminism in South Asian and Southeast Asian fictions.

Gurpreet Kaur (Ph.D.) has recently finished her Ph.D. in English and Comparative Literatures from the University of Warwick, UK. She did her B.A (Hons) and M.A degrees in English Language and Literature from the National University of Singapore. Her research, publications and conference presentations centre on postcolonial ecofeminism, South Asian and Southeast Asian fiction, film and gender studies.

Helen Tiffin Helen Tiffin is Honorary Professor of English and Animal Studies at the University of Wollongong, Australia. She previously held Professorships at the Universities of Queensland, Tasmania, and a Senior Research Chair at Queen's University in Canada. She has published numerous articles and authored, co-authored and edited ten books on post-colonial literatures, environment, and animal studies. Her current research is on problems and conflicts in conservation philosophy, policies and practices in a world increasingly affected by the pressures of climate change and human overpopulation.

Jose Monfred C. Sy has recently become an instructor at the University of the Philippines. He earned a Bachelor of Arts (Comparative Literature), summa cum laude, from the College of Arts and Letters of the same University. His research interests include the intersections between digital humanities and video game studies; ecocriticism and nature writing; spatiality and travel writing; and Marxism and children's literature. He is also a student and human rights activist.

Gabriela Lee has been published for her poetry and fiction in the Philippines, Singapore, the United States, and Australia. Her first book of fiction is titled *Instructions on How to Disappear: Stories* (Visprint Inc., 2016). Her previous works include *Disturbing the Universe: Poems* (NCCA Ubod New Writers Prize, 2006) and *La-on and the Seven Headed Dragon* (Adarna House, 2002). She received her BA in English Studies: Creative Writing from the University of the Philippines and her MA in Literary Studies from the National University of Singapore (NUS). She currently teaches literature and creative writing at the University of the Philippines. You can find out more about her work at www.sundialgirl.com.

Dang Thi Bich Hong was born in 1986. She grew up in Ban Nguyen Village, Lam Thao District, Phu Tho Province, Vietnam. After graduating from Hanoi National University of Education in 2008, she began her career in Hung Vuong University as a lecturer. She completed her Ph.D. in literary theory in 2016. She is the co-author of a book entitled *Postmodern Literary Criticism in Vietnam* (2013). Her publications include: *Teaching French Literature for Students of Philology Teacher Education: Difficulties and Solutions* (2012), *Paul Auster's City of Glass: Myth of Labyrinth in the Postmodern Period* (2013), *The Authorship of The New York Trilogy: Labyrinth of the Intellectual Game in Paul Auster's Novel* (2015) and *The Anti-Detective Fiction* (2015), *The Characteristics of the Plot of Detective Fiction* (2016). In addition to her research, she is a lecturer in literary theory and foreign literature at Hung Vuong University.

Hoang To Mai is a vice dean of the Foreign Literature Department, Institute of literature. Her specialism is the romantic period in American literature. She also writes about contemporary Vietnamese literature, and recently she is interested in Vietnamese literature from an ecological perspective. She is the chief editor of two books, *Romantic literature from* *other readings* and *What is Ecocriticism*. She is the author of some short story collections such as *White cloud menu, Hey, Blue shirt with white collar, A quiet song*. Many of her short stories have subtle ecological implications. She really wishes the Vietnamese people were more interested in the environment, especially writers and artists because their talents and fame can influence people's perception of serious environmental pollution in Vietnam.

Le Thi Huong Thuy is currently senior researcher of Vietnam Institute of Literature (Vietnam Academy of Social Sciences). She is the vice-chair of the Department of Contemporary Vietnamese Literature. She is the co-author of *Từ điển tác phẩm văn xuôi Việt Nam* [Dictionary of Contemporary Vietnamese Prose] (two volumes) (2006), *Tiểu thuyết và truyện ngắn Việt Nam từ 1975 đến nay* [Vietnamese Novels and Short Stories since 1975] (2012) and other books. She has published a number of articles in Vietnamese studying contemporary Vietnamese novels from perspectives of feminism, ecocriticism, and semiotics.

Nguyen Thi Nhu Trang is currently a lecturer of Department of Western Literature, Faculty of Literature, University of Social Sciences and Humanities (USSH), Vietnam National University (VNU), Hanoi. She was a student of honour program in USSH, VNU. She got a scholarship at Moscow State University (MSU/MGU), Russia in 2009. She earned her PhD in Russian Literature at the University of Social Sciences and Humanities, Vietnam National University, Hanoi in 2012. She teaches Russian Literature course for undergraduate students and some courses for graduate students such as 'Genre poetics of myth-novel', 'Theories of modernism and post-modernism', 'Film Narratology'. Her main research interests are national identity and religion in literature, migration and literature, spiritual deep ecology and religion. Her recent publication is "Master and Margarita by M. Bulgakov: a myth-novel". VNU press: 2016. She served as coordinator, ASLE-ASEAN coordinating committee for 'Ecologies in Southeast Asian Literature: histories, myths and societies' workshop, 26-27 January 2018. At present, she is the person in charge of VNU research project: 'Russian identity through Messianism in literature'.

Christian CULAS is an anthropologist at French National Center for Scientific Research (CNRS), Centre Norbert Elias, EHESS, Marseille, France. He spent 25 years of fieldwork about ethnic minorities groups and development projects research in Thailand, Laos and Vietnam. He has a thorough knowledge of lowland societies in Southeast Asia (Thai, Lao and Vietnamese) and highland ethnic groups (Hmong, Tay, Yao). Since 2005, He has specialised expertise in applied anthropology and sociology of ecotourism, sustainable tourism and about relationships between societies and the natural resources (Local knowledge and governance on natural resources management, Non-Timber Forest Products (NTFP), slash and burn cultivation, agro-forestry, and Conservation Agriculture). His current research focuses on the emergence of environmental awareness in Vietnam among urban citizens, peasants, NGOs and associations, industrial firms and civil servants.

Timothy F. Ong teaches at the Department of English and Comparative Literature, University of the Philippines—Diliman. He graduated with the MA in Literary and Cultural Studies from Ateneo de Manila University last 2017. In 2014, he was awarded the Asian Graduate Student Fellowship from the Asia Research Institute, National University of Singapore for his research on the tropics of eroticism in travel literatures in Southeast Asia. His research interests include postcolonial eroticism, tropical studies, geopoetics, ecocriticism, Philippine literatures, corporeality, and world poetry.

Nguyen Thi Mai Lien teaches at the Faculty of Philology, Ha Noi National University of Education, Vietnam. She graduated with the PhD in Literature of Asian Nations from Institute of Literature, Graduate Academy of Social Sciences, Vietnam last 1999. In 2014, She was recognised as an Associate Professor by the Vietnamese State Council for Professor Title in 2014. Her research interests include Culture and Literature of Asian Nations, Comparative Literature.

Index

A

A Lovesong, 5, 33
analogism, 111
animals' capacity, 17
animism, 6
Anthropocene, 4, 33
anthropogenic crisis, 109
ASEAN, 1, 2, 3, 4, 5, 7, 21, 155, 157
ASLE-ASEAN, 2

B

biodiversity, 33

C

children's literature, 4, 5, 49, 156
Chinese mode of worldview and the Western mode of worldview,, 6
concepts of risk and management, 4
Cyan Abad-Jugo, 5, 49

D

dirt theory, 73
dirty aesthetics, 4, 5, 83
Đỗ Phấn, 87

E

Ecocritical Mythology, 129
Ecocriticism, 2, 7, 69, 71, 157
ecofeminism, 69, 155
ecological imagination, 2
Ecological Injuries, 89
ecological poems, 5
ecological predicaments, 4
ecological wounds, 87
eco-narratives, 4
ecotopian fiction, 34
environmental consciousness, 3
environmental crises, 4
environmental justice, 5, 34

F

folk poetics, 6, 129
food crisis, 34
food security, 4, 5

G

Gone Wild, 16, 19
Great Apes, 10

H

Hinilawod, 6, 129
Hoya, 5, 73

I

imagining disasters, 4
indigenous epistemologies, 6, 129

K

Karl Marx, 3

L

Lê Minh Khuê, 6, 99, 108
Locust Girl, 5, 33

M

Margaret Atwood, 5, 33
metaphors, 5, 10, 14
Mouth of the River, 129
Mr. Mong's Story, 5
Myanmar, 1, 4, 21
myths and histories, 2

N

naturalism', 111
nature garden', 6
Nguyen Huy Thiep, 5, 73, 81
Nguyen Quang Thieu, 5, 59, 60, 61, 62, 63, 64, 65, 66, 67, 68, 69, 70, 71
nostalgia, 4, 5, 60, 68
numinous, 5, 49

O

orangutan, 4, 9, 10, 11, 12, 13, 14, 16, 17, 18, 19
Oryx and Crake, 5, 33

P

Philippine Daily Inquirer, 49
Philippines, 1, 5, 6, 129, 156, 158
postcolonial ecocriticism, 4
post-pastoral, 34
postwar Vietnam, 99
public sentiment, 9

S

Singapore, 1, 155, 156, 158
Sino-Vietnamese conceptions, 6, 111
social ecology, 3
Southeast Asian geo-space, 2

T

Taoist conceptions of nature, 6
The tropical Monsoon, 99
The Year of the Flood, 5, 33
traditional farming, 5, 73
Trauma, 21

U

urbanization, 87

V

Vietnam, 1, 2, 4, 5, 6, 21, 59, 61, 73, 99, 155, 157

W

war and post-war, 4
Western naturalism, 116
What the Orangutan Told Alice, 16, 19, 20

Y

Y Ban, 5, 73